VAGABOND VERSE

The Wheel of Fortune, from the *Carmina Burana*,
ed. J. A. Schmeller (Stuttgart, 1847)

𝔙𝔞𝔤𝔞𝔟𝔬𝔫𝔡 𝔙𝔢𝔯𝔰𝔢

SECULAR LATIN POEMS OF THE MIDDLE AGES

translated with
an introduction and commentary by

EDWIN H. ZEYDEL
University of Cincinnati

Wayne State University Press, Detroit

1966

Contents

8

Preface

THIS BOOK PRESENTS, in the original Latin and in English verse translation as faithful as possible in form and content, some sixty poems (one piece in prose) of the so-called vagabonds, dating approximately from 1000 A.D. to 1250. Since two other works still in print, and two now out of print, deal in whole or in part with the same subject, some explanation is necessary as to why this volume was undertaken.

John Addington Symonds' book, *Wine, Women and Song* (now out of print), contains about as many pieces as the present work.* It omits the Latin originals—the sparkling musicality of which no reader should miss— uses textual sources now somewhat out of date, and came out long before serious research on these poems had begun. The affinity between the vagabonds and the Renaissance, which Symonds senses, is no longer felt to exist. He includes only the *Carmina Burana;* the much earlier Cambridge Songs, known to him only from Du Méril, are only touched upon, and the vagabond works of the two fine poets, Hugh of Orléans and Walther of Châtillon, are unknown to him. His choice of selections is limited, although the translations are of high caliber. If the work of Symonds, that "woeful Victorian," is respected today as a minor classic, this is due at least in part to his position as a pioneer.

In Lindsay, *Medieval Latin Poets* (also out of print), about twenty-five of the poems in the present collection are translated. He gives them titles of his own, which, in the absence of the original Latin texts, makes it difficult to identify them, despite clues in the notes. His collection covers the entire Middle Ages, yet he omits

---

*Full titles of works often referred to in the text are cited in the Bibliography.

Walther of Châtillon, and his three-page introduction is hardly more than a preface.

Helen Waddell's work, in *Medieval Latin Lyrics,* resembles Lindsay's in that it does not concentrate upon the vagabond period but embraces the entire Middle Ages. However, in her translations she, like Symonds, does not pay much heed to the Cambridge Songs, nor to Hugh and Walther. She omits some of the best songs, for example, "The Deserted Girl" (p. 133 below). Sometimes her renderings merely paraphrase. For her knowledge of the Archipoeta she depends upon the first edition of Manitius (1913), meanwhile superseded by the second (1929); both have now been replaced by the Watenphul-Krefeld edition of 1958.

Although three important sections of the standard Hilka-Schumann edition of the *Carmina Burana* had already been out for a decade when the first edition of Whicher's work appeared, he makes little use of them in *The Goliard Poets.* He does not discuss Carl Orff's musical composition, *Carmina Burana,* which had already been known and much praised for twelve years. He also pays little attention to the results of recent scholarship. The important distinction between vagabonds and goliards is not made, so that the songs lose perspective. Whicher's brief introductions consequently do not clarify the origins and development of the vagabond movement. He also omits key poems and types of poetry found in the *Carmina Burana,* nor are the Cambridge Songs specially featured by him.

In view of these circumstances it seemed time for a volume of new translations of medieval Latin vagabond poetry—the most uninhibited and individualistic expression of the medieval mind—set off against the background of an introduction which endeavors to present this poetry as scholars now see it. Each generation can well afford to try its interpretative skill upon these poems anew.

A full introduction is an essential part of this book; it analyses and explains the vagabond poems as a product of the religious crisis of their time and draws distinctions between vagabond clerics, scholars, goliards, and gleemen, and traces relationships between the poetry of vagabonds, troubadours, and minnesingers. Studied in the Introduction are the prosody of the *carmina* and the lost music once an integral part of them; the reader is also informed about the chief manuscripts. The translations attempt to reproduce the prosody, and, through the original verse-rhythms, to give some idea of the nature of the music. They also represent all six types of vagabond songs, as illustrated in the division of chapters.

While the plan of the Introduction is my own, some parts of it are based upon the material in the works of Bechthum and Langosch, cited in my Bibliography.

The Commentary endeavors to trace references, especially the numerous biblical quotations so typical of the vagabonds, to clarify obscure allusions, and also gives the manuscript sources of the poems; the Appendix lists previous English translations.

It is a pleasure to acknowledge the valuable criticism of my erstwhile collaborator on several similar projects, Professor Bayard Quincy Morgan, the noted Stanford emeritus, who has read and improved both the translations and the Introduction. It is also a pleasant duty to express gratitude to Dr. Harold A. Basilius, director of the Wayne State University Press, for his interest in the project; to the readers of the Press for their valuable suggestions; and to the editor, Robert H. Tennenhouse, for his helpful advice and cooperation.

E. H. Z.

THE POEMS in the present collection, originating in France and Central Europe between about 1000 A.D. (or even earlier) and 1250, are all secular and the product of an international class of poets or rimesters known as *scholares* (or *clerici*) *vagantes,* also called *vagi*. They were the vagrom clerics—the vagabonds or vagrants. These designations should not be interpreted narrowly, although most of the poets, in their mode of living and way of thinking, represent typical medieval vagabond-age very well.

The earliest songs of these poets were written between about 990 and 1050. They still show the influence of the ecclesiastical chants used in the Roman Catholic divine service. During this early period, however, this poetry did not often attain full fruition. It is best represented by the first two poems in Chapter III (pp. 100 ff.), and the first five in Chapter VI (pp. 212 ff.). These are all from the Latin collection known as the Cambridge Songs, now in the library of Cambridge University, England, which consist of fifty poems, all intended to be sung or chanted. While the majority are spiritual and not the vagabond type, those included here are not religious, and, in most cases, are marked by realism and humor.

Much more mature are the vagabond songs of the twelfth and thirteenth centuries. They represent the finest secular Latin poetry, "a miracle of bud and blossom," as Helen Waddell remarks, and the most fascinating wealth of satires and student songs the Middle Ages produced. In this later stage vagabond poetry is set free from its dependence upon ecclesiastical and religious forms and themes, while still revealing its church-inspired origins. Occasionally too, its poets laid aside the anonymity they usually observed.

Although they did not form a unique class, either on

a national or an international level, the vagabond poets could be clearly distinguished in France and Central Europe, and to a lesser extent in England. Mainly, they were errant students and clerics, some having completed their education, others still hoping to do so, who through force of circumstances or by preference roamed about homeless, without office or preferment. They were particularly numerous in France. From the eleventh century on, students flocked from all directions to hear the most famous professors, at first in the *scholae publicae* of Tours, Liège, St. Gall, then in universities like Ravenna, Bologna, Padua, Paris, and Oxford. The highways saw more and more of such wayfarers. They were often penniless, although living was comparatively expensive and courses of study long. Many who had finished their ecclesiastical studies, in which the majority were engaged, could not secure the office they sought because of an over-supply of candidates and an accumulation of benefices in a few hands. Others again were too poor to complete their studies, like the poet in "A Plea for Clothing" (p. 73); or, as genuine *animulae vagulae*—vagrant spirits—to use a popular phrase of the time, they preferred vagabondage ("Adieu to Studies," p. 156, and "Love and Studies," p. 159) and philandering.

Being the work of such vagrom clerics, some of the songs are naturally only of average caliber, others however are the products of genuine poets ("Sleep and Love," p. 115, and "Invective against Venus," p. 149). Perhaps these were composed by older established clerics still young in heart.

In spite of their critical attitude toward their own circles and their looseness of living, the *vagantes* were not avowed enemies of established religion and of Christianity. To them the Church, with all it stood for, was an integral part of their lives, as it was to every European of that day. So firmly were they rooted in their faith that they dared take a detached position toward it. They actually harbored two souls in their breast—the soul of a medieval Christian who frequently quotes the Bible ("Song of the Vagabond Order" and "Vagabond's Confession," pp. 49 ff.), and that of a pseudo-classic devotee of Greek and Roman mythology to whom Cupid, Venus, and Bacchus were realities. Like the pastoral poets of earlier and later times, they preferred to give the characters of their poems fictitious names, so that their pages abound in references to Cecilia, Coronis, Florula, Glycerium, Paris, and Alcibiades. Ignoring their own times, they delighted in treating secular, profane matters quite apart from the world about them, but without meaning to indicate any anti-Christian or non-Christian tendencies. They did not reject Christianity; they laid it aside for the time being to indulge their other soul.

Nor were they an ostracized group, but educated clerics with all the privileges of immunity enjoyed by that class after tonsure. They paid no secular taxes, performed no military service, could not be tried in a secular court, and were entitled to alms.[1] Being exclusively under ecclesiastical law, they were not subject to the death penalty. Although in their verse they almost always assumed the role of miscreants and seemed to live by their vices, as a class they were not evil-doers.

But the attitude of the *vagantes* cannot be explained on personal grounds alone. It also grew out of the twelfth century religious crisis in Europe. There were bitter struggles between emperor and pope and deep-seated evils in the monasteries. The stern Cluniac reforms had caused a reaction and often achieved results not in keeping with the purposes of the order, which was guided by the Benedictine rule. The inroads of the Albigensian heresy were also a factor in the crisis. Consequently a spirit of criticism was cultivated and thrived in the centers of learning. Naturally the vagrants—the "have-nots" —were attracted by the unrest and took full advantage of it, as did many of their professors.

Diametrically opposed to these circles was a Middle High German poet such as Hartmann von Aue. He used old traditional material, such as the Oedipus-like legend of Gregorius, to affirm his conviction that contrition buttressed by faith can induce miracles.[2]

Proud as a class, the vagabonds acknowledged no intellectual superiors. Not possessed of office or responsibility, they felt free to criticize and ridicule usufructuaries among their "fellow" clergy through stinging satire and amusing parody. A subjective, individualistic spirit thrived among them as had never been seen before. They demonstrated a critical attitude toward a society that had not taken them fully into its confidence.

Bad as some of them were, the *vagantes* as a class should not be identified and confused with two other classes, the goliards and the gleemen. As individuals, to be sure, the *vagantes* and goliards were sometimes indistinguishable. Consequently their confusion is very common, as can be found in Thomas Wright's *The Latin Poems Commonly Attributed to "Walter Mapes"* (1841); in Ludwig Laistner's translations—*Golias: Studentenlieder des Mittelalters* (1879); and occurs as late as 1964 in Frederick B. Artz, *The Mind of the Middle Ages* (p. 330).[3] The term *golias* seems to occur as early as 913 A.D. in connection with one of the Church Councils of Sens, but this may be a clerical error and could apply to a council several hundred years later.[4]

Goliardus had become a term of reproach in the thirteenth century. It is already regarded as such in the poem "Vagabond's Confession" whose author, the Archipoeta, was himself a vagabond but not a goliard, and whose purpose was satirical. Usually the term is explained as deriving from the Latin *gula:* gullet. But this explanation is doubtful. In medieval Latin *golias* (never *gulias*) is a variant of Goliath, who is pictured as representing the devil. The supposed affinity to *gula,* even though erroneous, can be understood when one takes into account that these outcasts had a reputation for gluttony ("Vagabond's Confession," strophes 18, 19). *Golias* is also used to designate a fictitious bishop of the

Church, and this term became synonymous with *Eberhardinus,* a mocking reference to an epicurean archbishop of Salzburg.

In England the term "goliard" lived longer than on the continent; Langland and Chaucer used it. The "Confession" was familiar there and was used as a plea for the protection of the bishop of Coventry. England was also familiar with an "Apocolypse of Golias."[5]

The goliards, then, stood lower in the social scale than the *vagantes.* Still more inferior and less closely related to the latter were the gleemen, called *ioculatores* or *histriones.* Their purpose was to entertain; at ecclesiastical and secular courts, as well as at public gatherings, they appeared as acrobats, mimes, musicians, and jugglers. Sometimes they recited or chanted versified adventures composed by others. Socially they were completely déclassé—more so even than the goliards. Compared with them the *vagantes* were quite privileged. Moreover, the latter usually wrote their own verse—always intended for their own class or for higher classes.

The *vagantes* took a critical attitude in their verse toward the clerical circles they themselves belonged to, even toward their superiors. One might ask whether such attacks, which sometimes became vitriolic, were not indiscreet and indeed risky for a vagrant cleric whose living and future depended upon the goodwill of the hierarchy. Actually, this risk was not great, for the vast majority of the upper clergy were innocent of wrongdoing, also generous, and therefore they often sided with the vagrants in their criticism of a small minority. Indeed, they probably rejoiced at the witty, telling darts which the *vagantes* levelled at those who were disgracing the frock.

As we have seen, the vagabond poets were miscreants. This is brought out strikingly in "Vagabond's Confession"; the Archipoeta was one of the most notorious of the lot. He specifically mentions three vagabond sins of which he had been accused at the court of his patron, the arch-chancellor Reinald von Dassel: love, gambling, and drinking. He does not deny or abjure them but confesses the vagabond tendencies conducive to them. Indeed, these vices, especially the last two, continued to be the predominant ones throughout the Middle Ages, at least in Central Europe, even to the time of Sebastian Brant almost 350 years later.[6]

The vagabond songs have many typical facets. Among them are the versified pleas for alms of one kind or another; but it would be anachronistic to interpret them as mere begging. In the eyes of the supplicant poets, at least, they are justified demands for compensation for services rendered—quid pro quo—material pay for poetical favors. This comes out clearly in the latter part of the "Song of the Vagabond Order." Closely akin to such pleas are laments or satires on the stinginess of patrons whose gifts proved inadequate (see pp. 71, 73).

Nowhere does the spirit of vagabondage emerge more patently than in the songs of the tavern, in which gambling plays as important a part as excessive drinking (see Chapter II). In many variations the praises of wine and its stimulating effects are sung. Wine allays worry and grief and makes way for joy. Through it even the pauper acquires courage to defy his superiors. God Bacchus bestows eloquence and learning; he also sets love aflame. And hand in hand with the bibulousness of the tavern goes worship of another god, Decius, the deity of gaming. Even the abbot of Cockaigne (from the Old French land of cockaigne, or sugar cake; the German *Schlaraffenland*), addicted to Decius, gives fair warning that the god will denude the gambler (p. 87).

In "Vagabond's Confession," as well as in anonymous poems such as the "Song of Bacchus (p. 89), wine and love are linked. But in most cases the love song—a genre cultivated more assiduously than any other, and in some instances representing mere exercises—is restricted to love, or to springtime and love. As in the French troubadour song or the German minnesong, the Latin love song often begins as a song of nature and of the awakening of the earth after a cold, grey winter. But these songs are distinguished by the manner in which their singers— the vagabond clerics and students—represent love, and their attitude toward it.

The love whose praises these poets sing is sensual love. The object of their affection is often a peasant girl, not too young but not too old (p. 147). Usually she is not a girl of loose morals, nor is she a married woman involved in a real or imaginary clandestine affair. Her physical attractiveness, sometimes described in detail, her laughter, singing, and dancing, as well as her kisses, arouse her swain's passion among the wildflowers of a warm spring day. Never does he look for intellectual qualities in his beloved; he hopes rather to find voluptuousness. Coyness, reserve, and denial trouble him. Occasionally he is willing to wait until the girl has matured (p. 121). Sometimes the vagabond poet will use force to gratify his desires, whether the girl likes it or not (pp. 141, 173). He expresses his preference for a decent maiden over one of easy virtue or a married woman, but in "The Love of My Choice" (p. 147) he wants one who is not *too* chaste. The gem of all these songs is undoubtedly "Love and Sleep." Whicher, in *The Goliard Poets* (pp. 28 ff.), would like to assign it to Abélard, the French scholasticist and poet, himself perhaps a *vagus*. The most unconventional of the love poems, in an intricate meter and in the sequence form, is "Invective against Venus."

That the unrestrained loving of which he often sings may have evil consequences does not disturb the vagabond. If need be, he deserts the girl and creates a Faust-Margaret situation (p. 133).

At first glance the vagabonds seem to foreshadow the Renaissance, especially in their attitude toward life. However, we may question the claims of Symonds who, in *Wine, Women and Song* (pp. 174 ff.), regards the vagabond poets as forerunners of the Renaissance in their naive, careless mirth, their glorification of the body and senses, and their repudiation of "ascetic tyranny." Any parallels that can be drawn are only superficial.

To what extent the medieval vagabond lyric influenced the subsequent songs of the troubadours and minnesingers has never been determined fully. Ovid among the ancients, to a lesser extent Catullus, the Arabic songs, and the vernacular ditties of humble folk singers in many countries have left their mark not only upon the *carmina*, but also upon such French troubadour poets as Bernart de Ventadour, Bertrand de Born, Raimbaut Vaqueiras, and together with them, upon the German minnesingers, Friedrich von Hausen, Reinmar the Older, and Walther von der Vogelweide. But the imprint of the Latin *carmina* upon the Provençal and German singers is evident too. Indeed, some of the minnesongs of love and nature, as we shall find, seem like mere reworkings of such *carmina*. It is no wonder that besides bilingual poems ("Girl in Red Tunic") these German ditties are represented to no small degree in the collected *Carmina Burana*, "like dew on the grass of a heavy summer," as Helen Waddell puts it in her flowery way in *The Wandering Scholars* (p. 218). Some of these Middle High German songs are by such famous poets as the twelfth-century Reinmar the Older (a very noted German medieval poet), Walther von der Vogelweide, and Neidhart von Reuental (Hilka-Schumann eds. *Carmina Burana*, Nos. 147a, 151a, 168a). By the time they crept into the *Carmina Burana* they had probably become folk songs whose authorship had been forgotten.

The same conceits, the identical imagery prevail in French, German, and Latin songs. The presence of the nightingale (p. 105) and the lime or linden tree (p. 117) as devices establishes a clear relationship to German minnesong. The ideals of moderation and decorum, typical of the *minnelied*, are already found in the *carmina* (p. 125, strophe 9). So too the humble submission of the lover to his lady, far removed from the primitive domination of the male. "The Man's Wish," with his bold assertion that he expects the girl to meet him halfway, would seem to contradict this—until we reach the last strophe.

In some cases the Middle High German songs actually have counterparts among the Latin *carmina*. "A Song of Love" (p. 117), for instance, has a fairly close German parallel for strophes 1 and 3 in the *Carmina Burana* (No. 174a):

> Come, my dear, come, come to me,
> I entreat thee ardently!
> I entreat thee ardently,
> Come, my dear, come, come to me!
>
> Lips so sweet, of rosy glow,
> Come and cure my lover's woe!
> Come and cure my lover's woe,
> Lips so sweet, of rosy glow! [7]

Two other such pairs of even closer parallels are worth noting:

> Summer never did appear in the bygone days
> So delightful and so clear; flowers deck the braes.
> Birds that in the forest sing
> Join in pleasant chattering.

(*Carmina Burana*, No. 152, strophe 1, translated from Latin)

> I have never seen the summer appearing so delightful to me;
> With many pretty flowers the braes are decked.
> The forest is so full of song;
> The season is good for the little birds. [8]

(*Carmina Burana*, No. 152a, translated from German)

The other pair are:

> The noble forest is decked out
> With flowers and with leaves.
> Where is the whilom
> Lover of mine?
> He has ridden away!
> Alas, who will love me?

(*Carmina Burana*, No. 149 I, translated from Latin)

22

The forest is decked out
Everywhere.
Where is
My Lover staying so long?
He has ridden away.
Alas, who shall love me? [9]
(*Carmina Burana*, No. 149 II, translated from German)

As for the influence of the vernacular folk songs upon the Latin *carmina* and the German minnesongs, it is impossible to adduce any specific evidence. P. S. Allen, in *Medieval Latin Lyrics* (pp. 300 ff.), believes that such influence exists, but he, too, cannot point to definite instances.

Not all the conventional types found among the songs of the troubadours are clearly foreshadowed in the *carmina*, although the *dansa* appears in "To Springtime," and the *tensone* in "Phyllis and Flora." As a rule, the Latin poems take on the simple *canzone* form and, as already noted, remind us sometimes of Ovid or Catullus. In love-making they usually resemble the Middle High German type of *nidere minne*—the wooing of a maiden of humble station, not a lady of rank.

But there are differences too. In the most comprehensive English treatment of troubadour poetry thus far, *The Troubadours* by Robert Biffault (Bloomington, Ind., 1965), the Arabic influence of these songs is stressed. This influence and its non-Western nature are only slightly noticeable in the vagabond poetry we are considering here; it is more strongly felt in Italian and English verse. Moreover, the unrestricted sensual pleasure of the *carmina* is replaced in the troubadour and minnesinger by the spiritualization of love. The *vagantes* woo a maid, the troubadours mostly a mature lady of rank. The Latin poems usually are cast in a more carefree mold, given to mundane enjoyment. Considerations of morality and responsibility are not paramount in their attitude toward love any more than in their disposition toward drinking, gambling, and solicitation of alms. "The

Deserted Girl," in this setting, would not have attracted the troubadour's attention. The Latin *carmina*—not the work of an aristocratic caste, as are those of the troubadour type—picture no such narrowly circumscribed culture as we find in the formal garden of the courtly atmosphere, represented by the troubadours and minnesingers.

Related to the love poetry of the vagabonds are certain disputations and parodies which tend to effect a transition from the lyrical to the epic form. In an unusually long poem, "Phyllis and Flora," in which the two maidens are of *noble* birth, we are introduced to a disputation, in satirical, parodistic form, whether knights or clericals make better lovers. These two friends are alike in all respects, except that one loves a knight, the other a cleric. The poem begins idyllically enough in the month of May, but the argument that ensues becomes ever more heated and even acrid, until the disputants decide to leave the decision to Cupid. The fact that the cleric is declared the winner would seem to point to a clerical author—unless the poet was a very satirically inclined knight. Here too, sensual love is uppermost in everyone's mind. Flora, who loves the cleric, is frank to admit that the cleric's studies enlighten him not only on nature and the world, but also on love. It is the cleric, she asserts, who has taught the knight all he knows about love.[10]

None of the Latin *carmina*, except perhaps "Vagabond's Confession," have become as famous as "Phyllis and Flora." It served as the model for many similar works and was translated (or adapted) in English as early as 1595 by "R. S." (Richard Stapleton?), and published in George Chapman's *Ouid's Banquet of Sence* (London). In 1598 the English version appeared separately and in 1639 in a new edition of Chapman's work. The original and translation are also in Wright's *The Latin Poems . . .* (pp. 258 ff., 363 ff.). More recently, Symonds published a new partial rendering in *Wine,*

Women and Song; of the seventy-eight strophes, he translated the first twelve and fifteen later strophes.*
In the present edition almost twice as many strophes of "Phyllis and Flora" are offered.

Outright parody is found sporadically in numerous *carmina,* since parody is the very essence of vagabond songs. But it is not always as graceless and scorpion-like as Helen Waddell says (*Wandering Scholars,* p. 150). "Drinking," "Song of the Vagabond Order," and "Vagabond's Confession" are parodies of ecclesiastical orders which sprang up like mushrooms in the twelfth century; the "Song to Bacchus" is a parodistic prayer. The long "Leda Parody" of over fifty strophes, not included here, mocks the ancient mythological theme of Leda and the swan, not for ridicule but merely for the comedy that can be extracted from the subject—a glorification of very earthy love. Paul Lehmann, in *Die Parodie im Mittelalter,* treats the general subject adequately.

In the drinking and gaming songs there is often an almost blasphemous parody of convent rules and of the mass. Bogus tippling and gambling "masses" are solemnized, and gods like Bacchus and Decius celebrated as though they were truly divine. An altar is erected for Bacchus, the parody of a gradual is sung, and a prayer to Bacchus intoned. An introitus invites the celebrants to mourn misfortune in games of chance.

The most famous parodistic piece appears, like most of the twelfth- and thirteenth-century works so far mentioned, in the *Carmina Burana.* It is on p. 207: "Holy Gospel according to the Silver Mark." But this is more than a bold madcap parody. It serves as a weapon in the moral-satirical struggle against corruption among the upper clergy, against simony and the worship of material things. This struggle was much older than the Reformation or its immediate antecedents; an early symptom of it was the eleventh-century conflict between Pope Greg-

*Lindsay has also translated a generous portion of the poem.

ory VII and Emperor Henry IV on investitures, for it was essentially a conflict involving spiritual and temporal power.

A stock in trade of parodies like this was a play on words which everyone could understand. Mark (St. Mark) is associated with *marca* (a coin), *ara* (altar) with *arca* (money box), *numen* (deity) with *nummus* (money). Clever juxtaposition of quotations from the Gospels out of context serves to accuse even the Pope and the cardinals of greed, but at the same time appears to justify their improprieties. The climax of this hoax is the Pope's admonition to his followers to imitate his example. Here as elsewhere, however, the satire is directed only against abuses on the part of Church dignitaries, not against the faith itself.

Parody, then, developed into an instrument of satire against Church officials. But the "Song of the Vagabond Order" also shows such satire in a typical anonymous vagabond song. The two diatribes of Hugh of Orléans on the inferior fur coat, or coats, which he received from his bishop ("Curses on the Bishop" and "Dialog while Walking," pp. 70 ff.) are attacks of a purely personal nature—to be sure, against a high Church official—aiming at stinginess.

The vagabond poets, usually anonymous, did not always remain so. Two are known to us by their real names, Hugh of Orléans and Walther (or Guiot) of Châtillon; one by his nickname, the Archipoeta. These three, however, did not limit their poetry to the purely vagabond genre. Hugh also wrote miscellaneous poems of other kinds, Walther a long serious epic, and the Archipoeta a hymn to Frederick I (called Barbarossa—Red Beard), Emperor of the Holy Roman Empire. The trio lived rather early in the vagabond era. Hugh, born about 1095, and a generation younger than Abélard, was the oldest; the Archipoeta and Walther, both born about 1135, were two generations younger than he.

Hugh, with the well-earned and honorable designation of "Primas" or chief, was a native of Orléans; he pursued worldly studies and became a teacher. At various times he turned up in Amiens, Sens, Reims, Beauvais, and, in 1142, in Paris. He also journeyed to England. His death is set at about 1150. He attracted much attention with his verse. But undersized and unattractive in appearance—he compares himself in this respect with Zaccheus—he had a testy disposition and poor health, if we can believe him, and estranged many with his sharp tongue (p. 73). He spent his entire life as a vagabond, begging for alms and food. Indeed, poverty, whether a reality or not, became to him a badge of distinction, however unwelcome. In one of his poems he laments:

> A poet I who's poorer far than any other poet,
> I only own what here you see; 'tis well that you
>   should know it,
> And so I mourn and grieve the while you laugh and
>   scoff at me,
> But please don't think that I'm to blame for all
>   this poverty.[11]

A large number of Hugh's poems have been preserved, but only twenty-seven, found in an Oxford manuscript (Rawlinson G 109), were edited critically by Wilhelm Meyer almost sixty years ago. Some of the rest have been published imperfectly, many others not at all. Practically all we know of Hugh we owe to Meyer's researches. Hugh was irascible and proudly spiteful, but also witty, as shown in the attitude toward his bishop's cheap gifts. Other poems deal with drinking and gambling. In one he complains about a host who regaled him too liberally with wine, only to strip him of his meager funds in a game of dice. A typical vagabond and parasite, Hugh was once evicted from a canon's house, and was once kicked down a flight of stairs. Those who gave him liberally were rewarded with grateful, clever verse, but sometimes too with a request for more largess. The gift of a horse elicited a plea for fodder with which to feed the mount.

Hugh was a skilled craftsman and, according to Raby, the most original of all the medieval Latin poets.[12] Famed for his learning and wit, he is mentioned by such later writers as Serlo of Wilton (the friend of "Walter Mapes") and Richard of Poitiers. His language, with its plays on words, alliterations, accumulation of identical syllables, anaphora, and antithesis, the use of a single rhyme throughout long strophes, and violation of metrical rules to achieve novel effects, is striking and easily identifiable. His mode of expression is concrete and racy, his dialog lively. In his harsh satire against a wench who seemed to hold him in her grip (p. 237), he waxes Juvenalian. His Gallic temperament and riotousness make him outspoken on sexual matters (p. 241).

The Archipoeta, discovered by the German scholar Jacob Grimm in 1843 (not to be confused with two other medieval poets of the same designation), is known only by that flattering nickname, and until recently was a vague, shadowy figure. Like Hugh he was not a cleric. He once called himself, no less flatteringly, *vates vatum*—poet of poets. We do not know his birthplace, but in one of his poems, written about 1159 and addressed to his patron Reinald von Dassel, the imperial arch-chancellor and archbishop designate of Cologne (p. 247), he begs Reinald, as a "transmontane" (a Central European or German) to help him, who is also a transmontane. He seems therefore to have been a fellow-countryman of this high Cologne cleric. He was fairly widely travelled abroad and not unsusceptible to French influence, especially to that of Hugh, in meter and form.

The name "Archipoeta" is derived from an early thirteenth-century Göttingen manuscript (Philol. 170) which preserves eight of the ten (the other two are in Brussels) extant works, all written between 1159 and 1165.

The Archipoeta, of knightly rank but devoted to learning as well, was fortunate in having as his patron Reinald, who was the most influential courtier in all of Germany. The Archipoeta was much more prosperous than Hugh. As a result he was expected not only to provide entertainment, but to support his patron in his political ambitions, as a twelfth-century press agent, so to speak. Asked to write a heroic epic on the emperor, the Archipoeta couched his frank refusal in a poem. Instead he wrote a well-planned, dignified, but short encomium of the emperor, not without lauding Reinald at the end for making it possible for the emperor to reach Sicily on an expedition:

The arch-chancellor prepared the way,
Broadened the roads, and cleared away the brambles.[14]

In that manner the poet maintained his independence and self-respect, but at the same time did more to promote the policies of the emperor than he would have achieved with a lengthy panegyric.

Wagging tongues of envious rivals reported to Reinald, not without reason, that his protégé was indulging in loose living and sexual excesses. In "Vagabond's Confession," the jolly poem which enjoyed wide dissemination and fame throughout the Middle Ages because of its outspoken impudence, the poet cleverly succeeded in confounding his enemies. It is thought to have been written in Pavia, Italy, in 1163. Later, the Archipoeta got into more serious difficulty with Reinald because of some amorous adventures and was banished from his court for a while. Again he resorted to poetry for vindication, again in the form of a confession. "Jonah's Confession" is a frank admission of his own transgressions. It was so skillfully done, probably in the summer of 1164, that Reinald could not help but forgive him and restore him to his good graces.

In another poem, "Vision," probably of 1165, the Archipoeta achieved an even more striking result. He set out to persuade his patron that the monastery of St.

Martin's in Cologne had suffered an injustice which ought to be righted.

The dispute concerned a vineyard of three or four acres in Moselweiss (Wisse) which had been presented by the Coblenz provost Heinrich to the monastery and then, many years later, unrightfully taken away from it by a nephew of the provost. The abbot of the monastery brought the matter before Conrad, the Rhenish Count Palatine, but after some vacillation he decided against the monastery; then the abbot turned to the chancellor and archbishop Reinald. But since Conrad and Reinald were not on good terms and Reinald was cool toward the monastery, no action followed. Then the shrewd abbot used the Archipoeta as a mediator. The poem "Vision" contains the poet's plea in behalf of the monastery, with the result that Reinald was moved to use pressure and force Conrad to have the vineyard returned to St. Martin's monastery. The document recording the settlement of the dispute in this way has been preserved: *Privilegium Cunradi comitis Palentini de Vineis Wisse.*[15]

Henry Allen Moe has discovered and reported the striking case of a poem which directly affected and even made history: Langland's *The Vision of Piers Plowman,* in which "the actual language of some verses . . . became the law of England and later of the United States" with regard to the valid purposes of foundations and endowments.[16] In the same, but more limited, way the Archipoeta's "Vision," by interceding successfully in behalf of the monastery of St. Martin's, is a perhaps unique case in literary history in which a ruler was prevailed upon, by means of a poem, to take summary action in a public controversy.

Despite his favored, though at times precarious, position at court, the Archipoeta was one of the vagabond poets. Indeed, he has sometimes been identified with the mythical Golias himself. He did not reside with Reinald but wandered about: *folio similis . . . comparor fluvio labenti* ("like a leaf . . . I may be compared to a flowing river"), he says of himself in "Vagabond's Confession." He maintained his self-determination, lived loosely and often dissolutely. In the tavern he was happiest, given to begging and flattery, and was not ashamed of his vices. Under these circumstances it is surprising that, unlike Hugh of Orléans who undoubtedly has left some imprint upon him, the Archipoeta is not inclined to go to extremes or to offend good taste. Except in "Vagabond's Confession," moderation and tact usually characterize his language and style. Although he too liked an occasional tour de force in metrics and rhyme, his rhetorical tricks are not as studied and ostentatious as Hugh's. As a poet of possibly Germanic stock, he is not as temperamental and impulsive nor as racy as his Gallic predecessor, and his satiric barbs and his humor in general are less caustic. He has a warm, picturesque personality and leaves his readers in a relaxed, happy frame of mind.

Walther of Châtillon was born in Lille, in northern France, and was at first known as Gualtherus ab Insulis. He studied in Paris and Reims, was head of the cathedral school in Lâon, and then became canon in Reims. Soon he entered the chancery of the English King, Henry II (ruler also of a considerable part of France), befriending John of Salisbury and being present when Thomas à Becket was murdered. Later he took charge of the cathedral school of Châtillon, where he enjoyed so great a reputation that the name of the town became his sobriquet. In his later years he studied in Bologna and spent some time in Rome. Summoned home by archbishop William of Reims, he became canon in Amiens where he died of leprosy about 1200.

Walther's bulkiest work is the *Alexandreis,* a still readable epic of over five thousand lines, based upon an account of the life and exploits of Alexander the Great by Quintus Curtius Rufus, a writer of the Latin Silver Age. It was much read in the Middle Ages, sometimes rivalling the *Aeneid* in popularity, during an era when no consciousness of a break between antiquity and the Middle Ages existed. Of greater interest are the fifty-one lyric poems preserved for the most part in a manuscript in St. Omer, France (No. 351), and published by Karl Strecker in two volumes: pure lyrics in 1925, and moral-satirical poems in 1929 (the latter using also English, German, and Italian manuscripts).[17] Walther's fame also assured a place for some of his poems among the *Carmina Burana*, and in the British Arundel collection.

The moral-satirical poems comprise the most numerous single group. In the "Satire on Rome" he bewails the decay of the papal curia. Navigating between the pope and his retainers is like passing between Scylla and Charybdis:

> There greedy Scylla doth scold,
> And here Charybdis grasping for gold.[18]

In "The Venality of the Curia" he, like Juvenal constrained to write satire, paints a vivid picture of corruption:

> I shall resort to a song
> Of revolt against vices.
> Others [the clergy] set honey to entice us;
> They mingle gall with it.[19]

Especially popular was his "Complaint against the Upper Clergy," preserved in several sources. Most pessimistic is "The End of the World" where he foresees the triumph of the Antichrist.

With good reason it might be asked whether such satires should properly be called vagabond verse at all. Since satire and complaint against those in authority are part and parcel of vagabond poetry, the answer should be yes, especially since another poem of Walther (*Missus sum in vineam*—"I Was Sent to the Vineyard" [Strecker II, No. 6]) serves to point up clearly his position as a vagrom poet. Whoever, Walther exclaims here, strives for virtue, learning, and fame on his way to heaven is a fool, and will remain poor in goods and in love. Eating and drinking will serve him better. Wealth is to be striven for, but in moderation. A middle course between wealth and poverty is preferable. I quote a few snatches from this typical expression of the vagabond creed:

> Who for virtue strives and strains
> Slips into the depths.[20]

> O citizens, money must be sought above all.[21]

> Why do you honor books? [22]

> Hark, you who of Socrates
> Speak and write and think!
> Wretch, 't were better if you spent
> Time on food and drink.
> Yet if riches you disdain
> And reject inordinate gain,
> Find a middle course to steer, you'll be safe and free of fear.[23]

Walther, like Hugh, reveals an effervescent Gallic temperament. He goes much further than Hugh in his disregard of the rules of metrics and the conventions of style. He is an exhibitionist in this respect, an acrobat of rhythms, words, and conceits. But lacking the artistic instinct of Hugh and the Archipoeta, he usually fails to instill the lyric mood into his verse, be it secular or religious, and makes a display of his learning. He is not a poet who describes static conditions or situations, but action, epic movement. Yet, in spite of his shortcomings, he, too, possessed noteworthy gifts as a poet which are usually not associated with the age he lived in.

The name of one other poet will be found in this volume, "Walter Mapes," but it is in quotation marks. "Mapes," the Latin form for map, was an English contemporary of the Archipoeta and Walther of Châtillon; he studied in Paris and then served at the English court under Thomas à Becket. "Mapes" participated at the Lateran Council in 1179, and later became archdeacon in Oxford. He is known to have written the sharply satirical work on English court life (secular and ecclesiastical), *De nugis curialium* (courtly folderol). Other works, especially the "Confession of Golias," taken from the Archipoeta's "Confession" but addressed to the bishop of Coventry, were falsely ascribed to him. "Death to the Thief!" also belongs among these spurious poems. Another poem of "Mapes" is the "Apocalypse of Bishop Golias." As already noted, Thomas Wright has published the Latin poems attributed to "Walter Mapes."

All the poems in this collection, except those in ancient classical meters, were meant to be sung or chanted, but the melodies—with the exception of a few snatches indicated by the puzzling neumes, or musical signs, found sporadically in the *Carmina Burana* (see Commentary on "Deadly Love," p. 290), and some counterfactures of a later date—have unfortunately been lost.[24] Their starting point was liturgical music. *Poesia Latina Medievale* by Guiseppe Vecchi (2nd ed.; Parma, 1958) contains medieval music to poems 3, II; 2 and 13, III; 5, IV; 5, VI; and 6, VII.

Concerning the prosody of the songs, however, it is possible to be more specific. The poetry of the Latin classics was based upon the principle of quantity, in which each syllable is long or short by nature or position. But the closer medieval Latin came to the vernacular languages, which based their verse upon the principle of stress, the more completely Latin turned in that direction, too, ignoring the conventional Latin elision. The vagabond poetry of the earliest period (represented by the Cambridge Songs) still follows the pattern of the liturgical sequence, although alexandrines and adonics are found in it, too. But in the later stages, represented by the *Carmina Burana*, the word-rhythms are almost solely those of prose, except where changes have to be made for the sake of meter and in the case of hexameter and pentameter lines. The prosody of English and German today developed from that of medieval Latin.

The so-called vagabond line, usually in strophes of four lines each but often written as eight lines by dividing at the break in the middle of the line (the caesura), is in a trochaic measure and corresponds to the Old German couplet (see poems 1, 2, Chapter I). The first half, of seven syllables, is followed by the second half, of six, and the strophe has a fourfold single feminine (two-syllable) rhyme. An example of the rhyme from "Vagabond's Confession" is: *vehementi—menti—elementi—venti*. This gives the verse a playful, musical, pleasing, ring difficult to duplicate in English in which feminine rhymes are scarce. Rhyme, which the ancients used most sparingly and never as a regular device, is one of the most charming assets of vagabond verse, as it is of Christian Latin verse. The noted German classical philologist Wilamowitz von Möllendorf believed that only with medieval rhyme did Latin poetry attain its highest achievement. All the poems in the vagabond strophe, or in variations of it (for example in the first poems of Chapter I below), could be sung to the same melody. In the translations I have sometimes set a rest instead of the thirteenth syllable, or added a syllable.

The other meters used are simple too. Arsis and thesis (accented and unaccented syllables) alternate regularly, which makes reading and scanning easy. "Coronis," "Love and Studies," and the first three poems in Chapter VI, however, are composed as sequences, a form discussed in Chapter VI.

Hugh of Orléans is partial to the leonine hexameter, in which the caesura rhymes with the end of the line. He avoids elision, which makes his verses heavy from the point of view of classical Latin prosody. Rarely, if ever, does he use the vagabond strophe, then not in vogue. Occasionally he employs the elegiac distich, which couples a hexameter with a pentameter.

The Archipoeta makes occasional use of the vagabond strophe (pp. 58 and 256), but he too likes the rhymed hexameter and, as already noted, unusual rhymes which sometimes flout the rules. In "Jonah's Confession" (p. 250) the rhyming is carried to extremes. In each of the eleven strophes there is only one single rhyme.

Walther's metrics and style have been discussed above. He too uses the vagabond strophe when it suits his purpose. Generally he is a bold innovator, as in the poem "Hark . . ." (quoted above) where he adds a hexameter at the end of his vagabond strophe.

A peculiarity of the vagabond songs which crops up occasionally is what Wilhelm Meyer has called "Taktwechsel"—a change of beat or measure. Strophe 3 in "Farewell to Swabia" (p. 76) and every strophe in "Roundelay," where iambs replace trochees in certain lines, illustrate this. Meyer bases a prosodic theory and principle upon Taktwechsel.

While the original music accompanying the *carmina* has been lost, a modern composition sets to music twenty-five of the *Carmina Burana*. It was brought out under the title *Carmina Burana: Cantiones Profanae* and is the work of the German composer, Carl Orff. Completed in 1936 and published in 1937, it has since been performed with outstanding success in all parts of the world, including the United States. Written as a scenic cantata for stage presentation, it has also become part of a tryptych *Trionfi,* presented in Milan, Italy in 1953.

Orff's work consists of seven parts; it is partly orchestral and choral and partly for solo voices—soprano, tenor, baritone, and bass. As in my own arrangement, "Fortune, Empress of the World" is used as a prelude and the leading theme of the entire work; it also concludes the composition. Five of the *carmina* used by Orff are German, twenty Latin. Of the latter, nine appear in the present collection: the Prelude, "Vagabond's Confession," "Drinking," "The Abbot of Cockaigne," "Song of the Roasted Swan," "Joys of Springtime," "A Sport with Endless Charms," "A Song of Love," and "Girl in Red Tunic." In number of lines they equal about two-thirds of Orff's Latin selections. Orff's work is outstanding among contemporary musical compositions. He was quite successful in catching the spirit of the medieval songs.

Occasional reference has been made to the manuscripts in which the vagabond songs have come down to us. The oldest songs are in the manuscript known as the Cambridge Songs, already discussed. It was written in the eleventh century in England, probably in Canterbury, but is only a copy of a lost original. This was the work of a German who collected his material along the central and lower Rhine; seven of the songs deal with German emperors and princes, one contains a mixture of Latin and German. Another source for our collection, a thirteenth-century Vatican manuscript containing twelve songs, yields "Invective against Venus," one of the finest. A St. Omer manuscript (351), also of the thirteenth-century, contains thirty-three songs of Walther of Châtillon. An Oxford manuscript (Rawlinson G 109) contains much of what is known of Hugh of Orléans, while a Göttingen manuscript (Philol. 170) offers most of the little we have of the Archipoeta. The fourteenth-century so-called Arundel manuscript (No. 384, British Museum) contains twenty-eight songs, some of which are also found in the *Carmina Burana*. My poems "Coronis" and "Love and Studies" are in both manuscripts, while "The Love of My Choice" is only in Arundel.

This brings us to the most important of all the *carmina* manuscripts: the *Carmina Burana,* which, however, does not consist of vagabond songs alone. In 1803 the head of the Bavarian commission, charged with confiscating the monastic libraries, discovered this manuscript in the monastery of Benediktbeuren, south of Munich. It was found in a secret uncataloged cabinet among "forbidden" books, including Protestant works. Today it is Codex latinus 4660 of the Bavarian State Library. The librarian, Andreas Schmeller, published it for the first time in 1847, gave it its present name, and made a new (but unsatisfactory) arrangement of the songs, which had been scrambled when the manuscript was newly bound in the seventeenth or eighteenth century. Its subject matter is multifarious. It was probably compiled from many sources, chiefly French and German, and is international in scope.

Only 112 parchment leaves and seven loose sheets are left of this manuscript, which must have been considerably bulkier. It now contains fifty-five moral-satirical and historical songs, 131 love songs, thirty-five vagabond songs, and six religious plays. While most of the poems are in Latin, there are also German minnesongs (as was noted before—forty-eight in all), and bilingual songs: German-Latin and Latin-French. No author's names are mentioned. There are eight colored miniatures, the best that of The Wheel of Fortune, all the work of a single artist who also wrote a part of the manuscript. As has been indicated, neumes accompany some of the songs. The manuscript is now believed to have been written late in the thirteenth century in Benediktbeuren, commissioned by some wealthy or influential patron, perhaps a bishop or an abbot.

The new edition of the work begun in 1930 by Alfons Hilka and Otto Schumann, to comprise two volumes in three parts each, and now continued by Bernhard Bischoff in Munich, was not finished at this writing (see Bibliography). The new arrangement of the songs is by subject.

Little has been said here about the nationality of the individual anonymous Latin songs. Indeed, little is known about it, although in some cases we can be specific, as in the pastoral songs, or *pastourelles,* which are most likely French. Apparently, the compiler of the *Carmina Burana* was not at all restricted by considerations of nationality. As a matter of fact, even some of the Latin songs he found in German manuscripts may have been originally from France. It seems fairly safe to say, however, that the majority of the *carmina* are either of

French or German origin, with English a third and
Italian a fourth possibility.[25] Reference may also be
made here to "Shepherdess Taken by Storm" which states
the time as "before the month of May"; such an early
spring makes it likely that the song is of Provençal or
Italian origin. "Phyllis and Flora" has been called Italian,
but on dubious grounds.

Suffice it to say that the songs in this volume represent the Latin area of Europe, especially that covered
by French and German regions—in what proportion must
be left undecided, as well it may. For the *carmina* are
not a national product in the modern sense. They represent a cultural phenomenon of a much broader scope,
possible only in the Europe of the Middle Ages.

1. It was not unusual for a bishop to give money to a *vagus scholaris* or wandering scholar. See Helen Waddell, *The Wandering Scholars*, p. 237; and I. V. Zingerle, *Reisebeschreibungen Wolfgers von Ellenbrechtskirchen* (Vienna, 1877), pp. 8, 28. See also G. D. Mansi, *Sacrorum Conciliorum nova et amplissima collectio*, XXXIII (Graz, 1960), p. 237.

2. See Hartmann von Aue, *Gregorius; A Medieval Oedipus Legend,* trans. E. H. Zeydel and B. Q. Morgan (Chapel Hill, N. C., 1955).

3. Even in the medieval documents there seems to be confusion of *vagi, goliardi,* and *ioculatores.* In Appendix E of *The Wandering Scholars* decrees are cited from the tenth century to 1370 against those identified indiscriminately by one of these terms.

4. Mansi, XVIII, p. 324. But P. S. Allen (*Medieval Latin Lyrics*, p. 105) speaks of Irish goliards of the ninth century.

5. See Thomas Wright, *The Latin Poems Commonly Attributed to "Walter Mapes,"* pp. 1 ff., 71 ff.

6. See Sebastian Brant, *Ship of Fools*, trans. E. H. Zeydel (New York, 1962).

7. Chume, chume, geselle min,
   Ih enbite harte din!
   Ih enbite harte din,
   Chum, chum, geselle min!

   Suzer rosenvarwer munt,
   Chum unde mache mich gesunt,
   Chum und mache mich gesund,
   Suzer rosenvarwer munt!

8. Latin: Estas non apparuit   preteritis temporibus,
            Que sic clara fuerit;   ornantur prata floribus.
            Aves nunc in silva canunt
            Et canendo dulce garriunt.

German: Ich gesach den sumer nie,   daz er so schone
        duhte mich;
        Mit menigen blumen wolgetan   div heide hat
        gezieret sih.
        Sanges ist der walt so vol;
        Div zit div tut den chleinen volgelen wol.

9. Latin: Floret silva nobilis
        Floribus et foliis.
        Ubi est antiquus
        Meus amicus?
        Hinc equitavit!
        Eia! quis me amabit?

German: Grunet der walt
        Allenthalben
        Wa ist
        Min geselle also lange?
        Der ist geriten hinnen.
        Owi! wer sol mich minnen?

10. On the theme of the poem see my Commentary, and W. T. H. Jackson in *Zeitschrift für deutsches Altertum,* LXXXV (1954–55), 293 ff.

11. Poeta pauperior omnibus poetis,
Nichil prorsus habeo, nisi quod videtis.
Unde sepe lugeo, quando vos ridetis;
Nec me meo vitio pauperem putetis.

12. F. J. E. Raby, *A History of Secular Latin Poetry in the Middle Ages,* pp. 171 ff.

13. The arguments of Stach, von den Steinen, Schumann, and others that the Archipoeta was Gallic and not Germanic seem unfounded.

14. Archicancellarius   viam preparavit,
Dilatavit semitas   vepres extirpavit.

15. Quoted by Karl Langosch, *Hymnen und Vagantenlieder* (2nd ed.; Berlin, 1958), p. 338.

16. Henry Allen Moe, "The Power of Poetic Vision," *PMLA,* LXXIV (May, 1959), 37–41.

17. In 1937 A. Wilmart discovered some new poems that may also have been written by Walther; see *Révue bénédict,* XLIX, 121 ff., 322 ff.

18. Ibi latrat Scilla rapax
    Et Caribdis auri capax.

19. Utar contra vicia
    Carmine rebelli,
    Mel proponunt alii
    Fel supponunt melli.

20. Qui virtutes appetit
    Labitur in imum.

21. O cives, cives, querenda pecunia primum!

22. Cur libros honoras?

23. Audi, qui de Socrate
    Disputes et scribis,
    Miser, vaca pocius
    Potibus et cibis.
    Quod si dives fieri
    Noles vel nequibis,
    "Inter utrumque tene, medio tutissimus ibis."

24. On medieval musical settings, with particular reference
    to the German strophes of the *Carmina Burana,* see
    W. T. H. Jackson in *German Life and Letters,* n. s. VII
    (1953), 36 ff.; and Bruce A. Beatie in *Modern Language
    Notes,* LXXX (1965), 420 ff.

25. The Hilka-Schumann edition of the *Carmina Burana*
    gives full information on manuscript provenience and
    places of publication for every song. See the Bibliog-
    raphy in this volume.

O Fortuna

1.

O Fortuna,
Velut luna
Statu variabilis,
Semper crescis
Aut decrescis;—
Vita detestabilis
Nunc obdurat
Et tunc curat
Ludo mentis aciem,
Egestatem,
Potestatem
Dissolvit ut glaciem.

Prelude

THE WHEEL OF FORTUNE has been selected as the Prelude to this collection, as it was by Carl Orff for his composition *Carmina Burana*. It serves well as the vagabond's theme song because it associates gambling, one of the vagrom's chief vices and delights, with the idea that life itself is a gamble, a prominent tenet of his philosophy of life. Another song (in the same collection but not used by Orff) on the vagaries of Fortune contains the following typical couplets (see Commentary):

> The wheel of Fortune spins around
> While my estate is waning;
> But others toward the top are bound,
> Excessive heights attaining.*

The Wheel of Fortune

1.

Fortune's boon,
Like the moon,
Evermore with change is rife:
E'er increasing
Or decreasing;—
Our abominable life,
Sometimes rending,
Then amending
Playfully our derring-do,
In a trice
Thaws like ice
Poverty and power too.

* "Fortune rota volvitur: / Descendo minoratus; / Alter in altum tollitur, / Nimis exaltatus."

2.

Sors immanis
Et inanis,
Rota tu volubilis,
Status malus,
Vana salus
Semper dissolubilis,
Obumbratam
Et velatam
Mihi quoque niteris;
Nunc per ludum
Dorsum nudum
Fero tui sceleris.

3.

Sors salutis
Et virtutis
Michi nunc contraria
Est affectus
Et defectus
Semper in angaria.
Hac in hora
Sine mora
Corde pulsum tangite;
Quod per sortem
Sternit fortem,
Mecum omnes plangite!

2.

Fate so mighty,
Fate so flighty,
Like a wheel that must revolve,
Drives me mad,
Ah, I'm sad,
Everything will soon dissolve;
Under cover
All draped over,
Fate comes toward me for attack,
To her lash
Playful brash
I must bare my feeble back.

3.

Health and virtue,
Fate can hurt you!
Both of you abandon me.
My emotions,
My demotions
Suffer constant agony.
Snatch this day,
Don't delay,
Strike the lyre with grave intent;
How our fate
Fells what's great!
Come ye, join in my lament.

1. Cum "in orbem universum"

1.

Cum "in orbem universum"
Decantatur "ite,"
Sacerdotes ambulant,
Currunt cenobite,
Et ab evangelio
Iam surgunt levite,
Sectam nostram subeunt,
Que salus est vite.

CHAPTER I

𝔙agabond 𝔖ongs

THESE EIGHT typical vagabond songs (four by two known poets, the Archipoeta and Hugh of Orléans, and one falsely ascribed to the English poet "Walter Mapes"), written mostly between 1180 and 1220, the golden age of the medieval Latin lyric, reveal the vagabond satirically pretending membership in an order which he describes in detail and which parodies the religious orders of the day; brashly confessing his sins in an unrepentant spirit; begging proudly for alms; making sport of a high churchman; setting out from Germany to continue his studies in France (not without a note of homesickness); and heaping mock imprecations upon a petty thief. The vagabond is not ashamed of his vices, indeed he seems rather proud of them. He would "sunder goats from sheep," as he sings in the first of these songs, although knowing full well that the world rates him among the former, and insisting with tongue in cheek that he can play the game of life according to his own rules.

1. Song of the Vagabond Order

1.

At the signal, "Fare now forth,
Through the whole world haste,"
Priests go out in multitudes,
Monks no minute waste,
Levites sally forth and quit
Gospel's lucubration,
To our order all belong,
Which is life's salvation.

2.

In hac secta scriptum est:
"Omnia probate,
Vitam nostram optime
Vos considerate!
Contra pravos clericos
Vos perseverate,
Qui non large tribuunt
Vobis caritate!"

3.

Nos misericordie
Nunc sumus auctores,
Quia nos recipimus
Magnos et minores,
Divites recipimus
Et pauperiores,
Quos devoti monachi
Mittunt extra fores.

4.

Monachum recipimus
Cum rasa corona,
Et si venit presbiter
Cum sua matrona,
Magistrum cum pueris,
Virum cum persona,
Scholarem libencius
Tectum veste bona.

5.

Marchiones, Bavari,
Saxones, Australes,
Quotquot estis nobiles,
Vos precor sodales:
Auribus percipite
Novas decretales,
Quod avari pereant
Et non liberales!

2.

In this sect 't is written out:
"Test all things in season,
Weigh our life and judge it well
By your ripened reason,
So against bad clericals
Ever be alert
When they hand you charity
Less than your desert!"

3.

We invented charity,
't is our virtue solely,
For into our order we
Take both high and lowly,
Rich we take into our fold,
Those who live but poorly,
Whom devoted cenobites
Send a-packing dourly.

4.

We receive the roving monk
With his shaven pate,
Take the priest if he should bring
A matron as his mate,
Teachers also with their boys,
Men of high degree,
Scholars we like better still
Dressed attractively.

5.

Marchmen and Bavarians,
Saxons, Austrians,
All who have a noble urge,
I beseech you, friends:
Open up your ears and hear
New decrees we cherish,
That all misers bite the dust,
That the illiberal perish!

6.

Secta nostra recipit
Iustos et iniustos,
Claudos atque debiles,
Senio onustos . . .

. . . .

7.

Bellosos, pacificos,
Mites et insanos,
Boemos, Teutonicos,
Sclavos et Romanos,
Stature mediocres,
Gigantes et nanos,
In personis humiles
Et e contra vanos.

8.

De vagorum ordine
Dico vobis iura,
Quorum vita nobilis,
Dulcis est natura,
Quos delectat amplius
Pinguis assatura
Re vera, quam faciat
Hordei mensura.

9.

Ordo noster prohibet
Matutinas plane;
Sunt quedam fantasmata,
Que vagantur mane,
Per que nobis veniunt
Visiones vane.
Sic, qui nunc surrexerit,
Non est mentis sane.

6.

Proudly does our sect accept
Righteous and unfair,
Halt and lame and handicapped,
Aged who burdens bear . . .
· · · · · · · · · · · · · ·*

7.

Bellicose and peaceful souls,
Meek, crackpots a few,
Teutons and Bohemians,
Slavs and Romans too,
Men in stature undersized,
Dwarf and also giant,
Shrinking, modest characters,
E'en the vain, defiant.

8.

Hear the rules the order's made
Through its legislature,
For our life is dignified,
Sweet too is our nature;
Juicy roasts delight us more,
More would them we miss
Than a sack of barley grain
As a benefice.

9.

'gainst all matins we decree
This, our order's warning:
Certain specters stalk about
In the early morning,
Oftentimes they will dispatch
Visions weird and vain,
Therefore men who leave their beds
Early are insane.

*Text missing in manuscript.

10.

Ordo noster prohibet
Semper matutinas;
Sed statim cum surgimus,
Querimus pruinas,
Illuc ferri facimus
Vinum et gallinas.
Nil hic expavescimus
Ni Hasardhi minas.

11.

Ordo procul dubio
Secta vocitatur,
Quam diversi generis
Populus sectatur.
Ergo hic et hec et hoc
Ei preponatur,
Quod sit omnis generis,
Qui tot hospitatur.

12.

Ordo noster prohibet
Uti dupla veste:
Tunicam qui recipit,
Vadat vix honeste!
Pallium mox reicit
Decio conteste,
Cingulum huic detrahit
Ludus manifeste.

13.

Quod de summis dicitur,
Imis teneatur:
Camisia qui fruitur,
Bracis non utatur,
Caliga qui sequitur,
Calceus non feratur!
Nam qui hoc transgreditur,
Excommunicatur.

10.

So our principles forbid
Matins in any case;
When we once have risen, we
Seek a nice, cool place,
There we have a lackey bring
Wine and roasted chicken.
When we're gaming, we've one fear:
Luck that makes us sicken.

11.

Without doubt our order may
As a sect be rated
Since by folk of many kinds
It is cultivated.
Therefore let him, her and it
Be as members seated,
So that every type and class
May *en masse* be greeted.

12.

Notice this: Our rules forbid
Any change of clothing.
Who an extra doublet keeps,
Him we treat with loathing!
Soon he'll lose his overcoat—
Decius was averse—,
Next his belt he'll sacrifice
When his luck turns worse.

13.

What was said of upper clothes
Covers lower reaches,
Those who own a shirt, beware,
Shall not come in breeches!
He who walks about in boots
Finds all shoes outdated!
One who breaks this rule shall be
Excommunicated.

14.

Nemo prorsus exeat
Hospicium ieiunus,
Et si pauper fuerit,
Semper petat munus!
Incrementum recipit
Sepe nummus unus,
Cum ad ludum sederit
Lusor opportunus.

15.

Nemo in itinere
Contra ruat ventis
Nec ferat pauperiem
Vultu condolentis,
Sed spem sibi proponat
Semper consulentis!
Nam post grande sequitur
Malum sors gaudentis.

16.

Ad quos perveneritis,
Dicatis his, quare
Singulorum cupitis
Mores exprobrare:
"Reprobare reprobos
Et probos probare
Et hedos ab ovibus
Veni segregare."

14.

Hungry from a host's repast
Let no member drift,
If he is a needy man,
He shall beg a gift!
Any single penny may
Pave the way to many
When the gambler joins the game
With his *lucky* penny.

15.

No one on the highway shall
Fight the wind's oppression,
Nor endure his poverty
With a sad expression,
He shall always live in hope
As who sues in sorrow!
Luck will turn, for happiness
Follows grief tomorrow.

16.

So wherever you may go,
Give the folk your reason
Why you'd test the ways of men
In and out of season:
"I'd reprove the reprobates,
Good men I'd applaud,
I would sunder goats from sheep—
That's why I'm abroad."

2. Estuans intrinsecus

1.

Estuans intrinsecus
Ira vehementi
In amaritudine
Loquar mee menti:
Factus de materia
Levis elementi
Folio sum similis,
De quo ludunt venti.

2.

Cum sit enim proprium
Viro sapienti
Supra petram ponere
Sedem fundamenti,
Stultus ego comparor
Fluvio labenti
Sub eodem aere
Nunquam permanenti.

3.

Feror ego veluti
Sine nauta navis,
Ut per vias aeris
Vaga fertur avis.
Non me tenent vincula,
Non me tenet clavis,
Quero mei similes
Et adiungor pravis.

4.

Michi cordis gravitas
Res videtur gravis,
Iocus est amabilis
Dulciorque favis.
Quicquid Venus imperat,
Labor est suavis,
Que nunquam in cordibus
Habitat ignavis.

2. *Vagabond's Confession* (Archipoeta)

1.

Boiling in my very soul,
Wild with indignation,
I in bitterness of heart
Speak my declaration:
I am of an element
Volatile in matter,
Like a frail and withered leaf
Which the winds may scatter.

2.

Since it is the wise man's task
With consideration
Firm to set upon a rock
Home and its foundation,
I, a fool, may be compared
To a flowing river,
Always in the self-same bed,
Transient yet forever.

3.

Borne am I as in a ship,
Mate I lack to guide it,
As the bird flies through the air,
Aimlessly to ride it.
Bound by not a chain am I,
Checked by not a key,
I seek people like myself,
Find depravity.

4.

Gravity of heart is grave,
Anything but funny,
Jokes I love, they're sweeter than
Cakes of golden honey.
What Dame Venus may command
Is a toil of grace,
Venus never would reside
In a heart that's base.

5.
Via lata gradior
More iuventutis,
Implico me viciis
Immemor virtutis,
Voluptatis avidus
Magis quam salutis,
Mortuus in anima
Curam gero cutis.

6.
Presul discretissime,
Veniam te precor,
Morte bona morior,
Dulci neci necor,
Meum pectus sauciat
Puellarum decor,
Et quas tactu nequeo,
Saltem corde mecor.

7.
Res est arduissima
Vincere naturam,
In aspectu virginis
Mentem esse puram,
Iuvenes non possumus
Legem sequi duram
Leviumque corporum
Non habere curam.

8.
Quis in igne positus
Igne non uratur?
Quis Papie demorans
Castus habeatur,
Ubi Venus digito
Iuvenes venatur,
Oculis illaqueat,
Facie predatur?

5.

Down the highway broad I walk,
Like a youth in mind,
Implicate myself in vice,
Virtue stays behind,
Avid for the world's delight
More than for salvation,
Dead in soul, I care but for
Body's exultation.

6.

Prelate, you most circumspect,
Grace I would entreat,
It's a good death that I die,
Such a death is sweet,
O, my heart is wounded sore
When a lass comes near it,
If there's one I cannot touch,
Her I rape in spirit.

7.

't is most difficult indeed
Overcoming Nature,
Keeping pure our mind and thought
Near a girlish creature.
Young like me, one can't observe
Rules that are unfeeling,
Can't ignore such shapes and curves
Tempting and appealing.

8.

Who when into fire is pushed
Is by fire not scorched?
Whoso in Pavia stayed
Has not been debauched,
Where Dame Venus with a sign
Gives young men a shake-up,
Snares them with her luring eyes,
With her tempting makeup?

9.

Si ponas Ypolitum
Hodie Papie,
Non erit Ypolitus
In sequenti die;
Veneris in thalamos
Ducunt omnes vie,
Non est in tot turribus
Turris Aricie.

10.

Secundo redarguor
Eciam de ludo,
Sed cum ludus corpore
Me dimittat nudo,
Frigidus exterius
Mentis estu sudo,
Tunc versus et carmina
Meliora cudo.

11.

Tercio capitulo
Memoro tabernam,
Illam nullo tempore
Sprevi neque spernam,
Donec sanctos angelos
Venientes cernam,
Cantantes pro mortuis
"Requiem eternam."

12.

Meum est propositum
In taberna mori,
Ut sint vina proxima
Morientis ori.
Tunc cantabunt lecius
Angelorum chori:
"Sit deus propicius
Huic potatori!"

9.

If you led Hippolytus
To Pavia Sunday,
He'd not be Hippolytus
Any more on Monday.
To the bed of Venus lead
All roads every hour,
Only mid the many towers
Where's Aricia's tower?

10.

Secondly I've been accused
That I yield to gambling,
Yet when gambling strips me bare,
Then I can't go rambling,
For outside I quake with cold
While my heart glows white,
In this state far better song,
Finer verse I write.

11.

Thirdly to the tavern I
Must refer in turn,
This I've spurned not in the past
Nor will ever spurn,
Till the holy angels come
With a chant supernal,
Singing masses for the dead—
Requiem eternal.

12.

In the tavern let me die,
That's my resolution,
Bring me wine for lips so dry
At life's dissolution.
Joyfully the angel's choir
Then will sing my glory:
"Sit deus propicius
Huic potatori." *

*May God be well-disposed to this toper.

13.

Poculis accenditur
Animi lucerna,
Cor inbutum nectare
Volat ad superna.
Michi sapit dulcius
Vinum de taberna,
Quam quod aqua miscuit
Presulis pincerna.

14.

Loca vitant publica
Quidam poetarum
Et secretas eligunt
Sedes latebrarum,
Student, instant, vigilant
Nec laborant parum
Et vix tandem reddere
Possunt opus clarum.

15.

Ieiunant et abstinent
Poetarum chori,
Vitant rixas publicas
Et tumultus fori
Et, ut opus faciant,
Quod non possit mori,
Moriuntur studio
Subditi labori.

16.

Unicuique proprium
Dat Natura munus.
Ego nunquam potui
Scribere ieiunus,
Me ieiunum vincere
Posset puer unus.
Sitim et ieiunium
Odi tamquam funus.

13.

Through the cup new light bursts up
In my spirit's flare,
Nectar stimulates my heart
Etherward to fare.
Wine that in the tavern flows
Has a richer flavor
Than the watered stuff our lord's
Steward likes to savor.

14.

Certain poets strive to shun
Public spots and faces,
Choosing as their fixed locale
Secret hiding places,
Then they struggle, tug and toil,
Watchful not a little;
Though the works that they produce
Scarce are worth a tittle.

15.

Oft these poets fast, abstain,
Acting with decorum,
They avoid loud, coarse disputes,
Tumults in the forum,
And the while they would produce
Masterworks undying,
They themselves are snatched by death,
Ever vainly trying.

16.

Special gifts on every man
Mother Nature lavished;
I can never write a verse
When by hunger ravished,
If I'm famished, one small boy
Bests me in a trice,
Thirst and hunger I detest
Like my own demise.

17.

Unicuique proprium
Dat Natura donum.
Ego versus faciens
Bibo vinum bonum
Et quod habent purius
Dolia cauponum.
Tale vinum generat
Copiam sermonum.

18.

Tales versus facio,
Quale vinum bibo,
Nichil possum facere
Nisi sumpto cibo,
Nichil valent penitus,
Que ieiunus scribo.
Nasonem post calices
Carmine preibo.

19.

Michi nunquam spiritus
Poetrie datur,
Nisi prius fuerit
Venter bene satur.
Dum in arce cerebri
Bacchus dominatur,
In me Phebus irruit
Et miranda fatur.

20.

Ecce mee proditor
Pravitatis fui,
De qua me redarguunt
Servientes tui.
Sed eorum nullus est
Accusator sui,
Quamvis velint ludere
Seculoque frui.

17.

Special gifts for every man
Nature will produce,
I, when I compose my verse,
Vintage wine must use,
All the best the cellar's casks
Hold of these libations.
Such a wine calls forth from me
Copious conversations.

18.

My verse has the quality
Of the wine I sip,
I can not do much until
Food has passed my lip,
What I write when starved and parched
Is of lowest class,
When I'm tight, with verse I make
Ovid I surpass.

19.

As a poet ne'er can I
Be appreciated
Till my stomach has been well
Filled with food and sated,
When god Bacchus gains my brain's
Lofty citadel,
Phoebus rushes in to voice
Many a miracle.

20.

See, my own depravity
I have now confessed,
Disapproval of my sins
Have my friends expressed.
Not a single one of these
His own sins confesses,
Though he also likes the dice,
Likes the world's excesses.

21.

Iam nunc in presencia
Presulis beati
Secundum dominici
Regulam mandati
Mittat in me lapidem
Neque parcat vati,
Cuius non est animus
Conscius peccati.

22.

Sum locutus contra me,
Quicquid de me novi,
Et virus evomui,
Quod tam diu fovi.
Vita vetus displicet,
Mores placent novi;
Homo videt faciem,
Sed cor patet Iovi.

23.

Iam virtutes diligo,
Viciis irascor,
Renovatus animo
Spiritu renascor,
Quasi modo genitus
Novo lacte pascor,
Ne sit meum amplius
Vanitatis vas cor.

24.

Electe Colonie,
Parce penitenti,
Fac misericordiam
Veniam petenti
Et da penitenciam
Culpam confitenti!
Feram, quicquid iusseris,
Animo libenti.

21.

In my master's presence now
Let that man appear,
And as in the Lord's own words
We from scripture hear,
He may cast a stone at me,
Sparing not the poet,
If of sin he's innocent
And perhaps may know it.

22.

I have said against myself
All the bad I knew,
Of the poison deep inside
I am rid, as spew.
Former ways displease me now,
New paths I must start;
Man sees externalities,
Jove discerns the heart.

23.

Now I love the virtues all,
Vices I despise,
With a spirit that's renewed
Higher I may rise,
Like an infant newly born,
Fresh milk stills my hunger,
So my heart holds in its vat
Vanity no longer.

24.

New archbishop of Cologne,
Spare the penitent,
Show your pity for a man
On forgiveness bent.
Name the penance to absolve
Sins he will confess!
I'll endure what'ever you say,
Yea, with willingness.

25.

Parcit enim subditis
Leo rex ferarum
Et est erga subditos
Immemor irarum.
Et vos idem facite,
Principes terrarum!
Quod caret dulcedine,
Nimis est amarum.

3. Pontificum spuma

Pontificum spuma, fex cleri, sordida struma,
Qui dedit in bruma michi mantellum sine pluma!

4. Hoc indumentum

"Hoc indumentum tibi quis dedit? An fuit emptum?
Estne tuum?"—"Nostrum. Sed qui dedit, abstulit
ostrum."—
"Quis dedit hoc munus?"—"Presul michi prebuit unus."—
"Qui dedit hoc munus, dedit hoc in munere funus.
Quid valet in bruma clamis absque pilo, sine pluma?
Cernis adesse nives, moriere gelu neque vives."

25.

E'en the lion, king of beasts,
Spares subordinates,
Wrath that they may stir in him
Promptly he forgets.
This, O you who rule the earth,
Be your guide, 't were fitter!
For whatever lacks some sweet
Men find all too bitter.

3. *Curses on the Bishop* (Hugh of Orléans)

Bishop, you're scummy, the dregs of the clergy, your
                              throat has a crop.
Winter is here and you gave me a coat without fur on
                              the top.

4. *Dialog while Walking* (Hugh of Orléans)

"Where did you pick up that coat? It must have been
                              bought for a song!
Is it your own?"—"Yes, it is! But who gave, took the collar
                              along."
"Who would present such a gift?"—" 't was the bishop
                              who made the donation!"—
"The fellow who gave it, I swear, was planning your
                              sheer ruination!
Who would have use for a coat sans fur—with a lining so
                              old?
Just let a blizzard approach, you'll perish of wind and of
                              cold."

5. Primas pontifici

Primas pontifici: "Bene quod sapis audio dici,
Ut fama teste probitas est magna penes te.
Conspicuus veste, bene cenas, vivis honeste.
Et bene si vivis et das bene de genetivis,
Ut non egrotes, bene convenit, ut bene potes."

6. Exul ego clericus

1.
Exul ego clericus
Ad laborem natus
Tribulor multociens
Paupertati datus.

2.
Litterarum studiis
Vellem insudare,
Nisi quod inopia
Cogit me cessare.

3.
Ille meus tenuis
Nimis est amictus;
Sepe frigus pacior
Calore relictus.

4.
Interesse laudibus
Non possum divinis,
Nec misse nec vespere,
Dum cantetur finis.

5.
Decus N.,
Dum sitis insigne,
Postulo suffragia
De vobis iam digne.

5. *Bishop, Drink!* (Hugh of Orléans)

The Primas to the prelate: "You're wise! I've heard men
tell it,
Your probity and fame add glory to your name.
You're elegantly dressed, eat well, your life is blest.
Since you live lavishly, with great virility,
Be sure you drink your fill so that you'll not fall ill."

6. *A Plea for Clothing*

1.

I, a cleric on the loose,
Given to tribulation,
Am for toil and travail born,
Poverty's my ration.

2.

For the arts and literature
I possess a yearning,
Still, my indigence compels
Me to cease from learning.

3.

All my clothing that I wear,
Frail it is and torn;
Oftentimes I suffer cold
Since of warmth I'm shorn.

4.

Cannot praise the Lord in church
While my knees are bending,
Cannot hear the masses out,
Nor the vespers' ending.

5.

Worthy lord of N., kind sir,
Since your fame shines brightly,
I beseech a little gift
From your grace politely.

6.

Ergo mentem capite
Similem Martini,
Vestibus induite
Corpus peregrini,

7.

Ut vos Deus transferat
Ad regna polorum!
Ibi dona conferunt
Vobis beatorum.

7. Hospita in Gallia

1.

Hospita in Gallia
Nunc me vocant studia;
Vadam ergo,
Flens a tergo
Socios relinquo.
Plangite, discipuli,
Lugubris discidii
Tempore propinquo!

2.

O consortes studii,
Deprecor, valete,
Quos benigne colui,
Filii, dolete!
Classem solvo litore,
Remigo, videte,
Proficiscor peregre,
Socium deflete!

6.

Take St. Martin's attitude,
Never mean or shoddy,
Give the pilgrim-scholar clothes,
Cover up his body .

7.

So may God transport your soul
Into realms eternal,
May the gift of saints be yours
In God's heaven supernal.

7. *Farewell to Swabia*

1.

To the distant clime of Gaul
Studies beckon me and call;
So while grieving
Friends I'm leaving:
All must stay behind.
Mourn, my pals, the while I roam,
Soon I'll be forsaking home,
Now 't will not be long!

2.

Fellows who my studies shared,
Hear now my farewell,
Comrades all for whom I cared,
Let your sorrow swell!
From the shore I take my skiff,
Witness how I row,
I set out for foreign ports,
Weep, friends, as I go.

3.

Versibus eleicis
Cetum discipulorum
Commendo cum lacrimis
Iam deo deorum:
Foveat et protegat
Magnos cum pusillis,
Custodiat et maneat
Perenniter cum illis!

4.

Rorate, mea lumina,
Super gregem meum!
Si concedent numina,
Revisitabo eum
Et sicut a principio
Super hunc regnabo,
Si non in exilio
Miser expirabo.

5.

Vale, dulcis patria,
Suavis Suevorum Suevia,
Salve, dilecta Francia,
Philosophorum curia!
Suscipe discipulum
In te peregrinum,
Quem post dierum circulum
Remittes Socratinum!

6.

In manus eius animam
Et spiritum commendo,
Qui se dedit in victimam
Pro me redimendo
Et verus innotuit
Deus resurgendo,
De Bosram tinctis vestibus
Celos ascendendo.

3.

With lamenting lines like these,
Tearful I commend
To Him who rules o'er deities
Each and every friend:
May He cherish and protect
Great and small together,
O may he guard and stay with them
In every kind of weather!

4.

Mine eyes, O let your teardrops flow,
O'er my flock they'll rain!
If the gods decree it so
I'll see them all again,
And then, as at the start, I will
Rule them as their sire—
If as exile wandering
I do not expire.

5.

Dear my fatherland, to you,
Sweet Swabian Swabia, adieu,
Beloved France to which I roam,
All hail! Philosophy's your home!
Take the foreign student up
To your bosom, please,
And when the time's ripe, send him back
Well trained like Socrates!

6.

I now commend my soul, my breath
To God's own custody
Who once relinquished life in death
To deliver me;
As the true God was He known
By His resurrection,
And crimson-robed from Bozrah He
Rose in heaven's direction.

7.

Duplex est divisio,
Una substanciarum,
Que fit in hoc discidio,
Sed non animarum.
Vobiscum sum, dum vixero,
Spiritu presente,
Licet absens abero
Corpore, non mente.

8.

Ad urbem sapiencie
Denuo festino:
Spiritus sciencie
Assit peregrino,
Visitet, illuminet
Mentem imperitam,
Ut misticam sufficiam
Mercari margaritam!

8. Raptor mei pilei

1.

Raptor mei pilei
Morte moriatur,
Mors sit subitanea
Nec prevideatur,
Et pena continua
Post mortem sequatur,
Nec campis Elysiis
Post Lethen fruatur!

7.

Twofold separations smart,
One is physical:
't will come when later I go hence
't is not spiritual.
I have for you the while I live
Heartfelt recollection;
Though I'm gone, I'll take away
Body, not affection.

8.

To Wisdom's city of renown
Haste I, as I have said:
Learning's spirit, settle down
Upon this exile's head;
May it come enlightening me,
Who've so much to learn,
And worthy may I be adjudged
The mystic pearl to earn.

8. Death to the Thief! ("Walter Mapes")

1.

May the snatcher of my cap
Die a death, the rat,
May his death be sudden too,
Unforeseen at that,
Him may constant punishment
When he's dead, annoy,
Nor shall after Lethe he
The Elysian fields enjoy!

2.

Raptor mei pilei
Seva morte cadat,
Illum febris, scabies
Et tabes invadat,
Hunc de libro Dominus
Vite sue radat,
Hunc tormentis Eacus
Cruciandum tradat!

3.

Eius vita brevis sit
Pessimusque finis,
Nec vivat feliciter
Hic diebus binis,
Laceret hunc Cerberus
Dentibus caninis,
Laceratum gravius
Torqueat Erinys!

4.

Excommunicatus sit
Agro vel in tecto,
Nullus eum videat
Lumine directo,
Solus semper sedeat
Similis deiecto,
Hinc penis Tartareis
Cruciet Alecto!

5.

Hoc si quis audierit
Excommunicamen
Et non observaverit
Presulis examen,
Nisi resipuerit
Corrigens peccamen,
Anathema fuerit,
Fiat, fiat! Amen.

2.

May the snatcher of my cap
Grim death undergo,
May the plague and leprosy
And fever lay him low,
Him may God from life's big book
Cancel and erase,
Him may Aeacus, the judge,
Mark for tortures base!

3.

Let his life endure not long,
The ending gruesome be,
Let him live but for two days,
All unhappily;
Cerberus shall rip him up
With his canine teeth;
May the Furies tear him worse,
Tortures too bequeath!

4.

He shall suffer where he goes
Excommunication,
No one shall behold him in
Bright illumination,
He shall always sit alone
Like a soul dejected,
May Alecto's pains of hell
'gainst him be directed!

5.

If of this horrendous ban
Anyone has heard
Yet denies obedience
To our master's word,
He, unless he would repent,
Right his wrong and flee it,
He will be anathema!
Yes, amen, so be it!

1. In taberna quando sumus

1.

In taberna quando sumus,
Non curamus, quid sit humus,
Sed ad ludum properamus,
Cui semper insudamus.
Quid agatur in taberna,
Ubi nummus est pincerna,
Hoc est opus, ut queratur,
Sed quid loquar, audiatur!

CHAPTER II

𝔖𝔬𝔫𝔤𝔰 𝔬𝔣 𝔱𝔥𝔢 𝔗𝔞𝔟𝔢𝔯𝔫

THESE FIVE drinking songs, all probably written in the thirteenth century or shortly before, reveal a brash attitude of outspoken, unashamed devotion to wine, women, and song—always in a good-humored, merry mood. Gambling is recognized as going hand in hand with these carefree pursuits. A fictitious abbot, who was probably quite real to the poet and who seems to have hailed from France but was somehow repatriated in Germany, participates in the revels. Bacchus, the "lofty deity," is addressed with all the reverence due an omnipotent god. But feasting, too, goes with drinking, as the jolly "Song of the Roasted Swan" (a delicacy unknown today) shows. This song is the more poignant because it is voiced by the poor fowl itself.

1. *Drinking*

1.

When we're in the tavern drinking,
Of the earth we're far from thinking,
But we haste to games and betting,
Over which we're always sweating.
What goes on in taverns many,
Where the butler is the penny,
That to ascertain we seek,
Listen now to what I speak!

2.

Quidam ludunt, quidam bibunt,
Quidam indiscrete vivunt.
Sed in ludo qui morantur,
Ex his quidam denudantur,
Quidam ibi vectiuntur,
Quidam saccis induuntur.
Ibi nullus timet mortem,
Sed pro Baccho mittunt sortem.

3.

Primo pro nummata vini,
Ex hac bibunt libertini,
Semel bibunt pro captivis,
Post hec bibunt ter pro vivis,
Quater pro Chriscianis cunctis,
Quinquies—pro fidelibus defunctis,
Sexies—pro sororibus vanis,
Sepcies—pro militibus silvanis,

4.

Occies—pro fratribus perversis,
Novies—pro monachis dispersis,
Decies—pro navigantibus,
Undecies—pro discordantibus,
Duodecies—pro penitentibus,
Tredecies—pro iter agentibus.
Tam pro papa quam pro rege
Bibunt omnes sine lege.

5.

Bibit hera, bibit herus,
Bibit miles, bibit clerus,
Bibit ille, bibit illa,
Bibit servus cum ancilla,
Bibit velox, bibit piger,
Bibit albus, bibit niger,
Bibit constans, bibit vagus,
Bibit rudis, bibit magus.

2.

Some will gamble, some carouse,
Some will live like foolish sows.
Some, by gamblers' ways deluded,
Oftentimes are thus denuded,
Some new garments may receive,
Others will in sackcloth leave.
Death these people fear no jot,
They with Bacchus cast their lot.

3.

First they drink to who will pay?
Then the rounds get under way:
Once to who in prison fret,
Thrice to all men living yet,
Fourth, to Christians far and wide,
Fifth—to faithful ones who've died,
Sixth—to empty-headed daughters,
Seventh—to militant marauders,

4.

Eighth—to brotherhoods perverse,
Ninth—to monks who oft disperse,
Tenth—to those in navigation,
Eleventh—who like altercation,
Twelfth—to all the penitent,
Thirteenth—those on travel bent.
Now to pope and then to king
All drink, never questioning.

5.

Lady mine drinks, so the master,
Soldiers drink, so does the pastor,
He drinks, she drinks, as I've said,
Serving man and serving maid,
Speedsters drink, the sloths respond,
Brunets too and so the blond,
Scatterbrains, the constant brood,
Wise men drink, as do the rude.

6.

Bibit pauper et egrotus,
Bibit exul et ignotus,
Bibit puer, bibit canus,
Bibit presul et decanus,
Bibit soror, bibit frater,
Bibit anus, bibit mater.
Bibit ista, bibit ille,
Bibunt centum, bibunt mille.

7.

Parum sescente nummate
Durant, cum immoderate
Bibunt omnes sine meta,
Quamvis bibant mente leta.
Sic nos rodunt omnes gentes,
Et sic erimus egentes.
Qui nos rodunt, confundantur
Et cum iustis non scribantur!

2. Ego sum abbas

Ego sum abbas Cucaniensis
Et consulium meum est cum bibulis,
Et in secta Decii voluntas mea est,
Et qui mane me quesierit in taberna,
Post vesperam nudus egredietur,
Et sic denudatus veste clamabit:

Wafna, wafna!
Quid fecisti sors turpissima?
Nostre vite gaudia,
Abstulisti omnia!

6.

Paupers drink, as do the ill,
Exiles too and morons will,
Young lad, greybeard drink their measures
Such as dean or bishop treasures,
Sister drinks and so does brother,
Old hags drink, so does the mother,
He drinks, she drinks cups untold,
A hundredfold, a thousandfold.

7.

Coins six hundred soon are spent
Where such drinking's prevalent,
Where men drink with boundless folly,
Though while drinking they are jolly.
People gnaw at us and blame us,
Poverty will soon defame us.
May our carping critics sicken,
From the righteous ranks be stricken!

2. The Abbot of Cockaigne

I am the abbot well-known of Cockaigne
And this is my counsel in case you're a toper,
In the sect of god Decius this is my will:
Whoever may seek me in inns of a morning,
When sundown is come he shall issue all naked,
And thus stripped of garments, he shall complain:

Wafna, wafna!
Fate most shameful, what, pray, have you done?
Joys that by our lives are spun
You have taken, every one!

3. Bacche, benevenias

1.

Bacche, benevenias
Gratus et optatus,
Per quem noster animus
Fit letificatus!
    Istud vinum, bonum vinum,
    Vinum generosum
    Reddit virum curialem,
    Probum, animosum.

2.

Bacchus lenis, leniens
Curas et dolores
Confert iocum, gaudia,
Risus et amores.
    Istud vinum, bonum vinum,
    Vinum generosum
    Reddit virum curialem,
    Probum, animosum.

3.

Bacchus forte superans
Pectora virorum
In amorem concitat
Animos eorum.
    Istud vinum, bonum vinum,
    Vinum generosum
    Reddit virum curialem,
    Probum, animosum.

4.

Bacchus sepe visitans
Mulierum genus
Facit eas subditas
Tibi, o tu Venus.
    Istud vinum, bonum vinum,
    Vinum generosum
    Reddit virum curialem,
    Probum, animosum.

3. *Song to Bacchus*

1.

Bacchus, welcome, we exclaim,
We are glad you're here,
For in you our minds and hearts
Find delight and cheer!
 O this wine, this wine so good,
 Wine of purest gold,
 Gives a man a courtly touch,
 Makes him sound and bold.

2.

Gentle Bacchus, softening
Grief and doleful care,
Offers jest and joy and love,
Laughter debonair.
 O this wine, this wine so good,
 Wine of purest gold,
 Gives a man a courtly touch,
 Makes him sound and bold.

3.

Bacchus, conquering by force
Man's uneasy breast,
Sparks his sensibility
With a lover's zest.
 O this wine, this wine so good,
 Wine of purest gold,
 Gives a man a courtly touch,
 Makes him sound and bold.

4.

Bacchus, often visiting
Women's noted genus,
Serves in steadfast fealty
You alone, O Venus.
 O this wine, this wine so good,
 Wine of purest gold,
 Gives a man a courtly touch,
 Makes him sound and bold.

5.

Bacchus venas penetrans
Calido liquore
Facit eas igneas
Veneris ardore.
  Istud vinum, bonum vinum,
  Vinum generosum
  Reddit virum curialem,
  Probum, animosum.

6.

Bacchus mentem femine
Solet hic lenire,
Cogit eam cicius
Viro consentire.
  Istud vinum, bonum vinum,
  Vinum generosum
  Reddit virum curialem,
  Probum, animosum.

7.

Bacchus numen faciens
Hominem iucundum
Reddit eum pariter
Doctum et facundum.
  Istud vinum, bonum vinum,
  Vinum generosum
  Reddit virum curialem,
  Probum, animosum.

8.

Bacche, deus inclite,
Omnes hic adstantes
Leti sumus munera
Tua prelibantes.
  Istud vinum, bonum vinum,
  Vinum generosum
  Reddit virum curialem,
  Probum, animosum.

5.

Bacchus lets his fiery stream
Through our arteries flow,
Makes them burn and sear and scorch
With Dame Venus' glow.
O this wine, this wine so good,
Wine of purest gold,
Gives a man a courtly touch,
Makes him sound and bold.

6.

Bacchus too is wont to melt
Women's mind and bent,
Making them more prone when man
Beg for their consent.
O this wine, this wine so good,
Wine of purest gold,
Gives a man a courtly touch,
Makes him sound and bold.

7.

Bacchus can make gods of men
Socially inclined,
Give them learning, eloquence,
Powers of the mind.
O this wine, this wine so good,
Wine of purest gold,
Gives a man a courtly touch,
Makes him sound and bold.

8.

Bacchus, lofty deity,
All who tarry here
Welcome your libations, god,
Pledging bounteous cheer.
O this wine, this wine so good,
Wine of purest gold,
Gives a man a courtly touch,
Makes him sound and bold.

4. Simus hic sedentes

1.

Simus hic sedentes
Sicut conferentes,
In omnibus gaudentes,
Nullum offendentes,
Sed leti,
Faceti
Concinentes!

2.

Ergo infundatur!
Sic cor iucundatur,
Tristicia fugatur,
Plausus innovatur
Et lete,
Facete
Concinatur!

3.

Virgo generosa
Dei speciosa,
Pre ceteris formosa,
Paradisi rosa,
Sit genti
Bibenti
Graciosa!

4.

Socii, bibamus,
Cifum capiamus,
Hilariter vivamus!
Sic valet, ut potamus.
Habunde,
Iucunde
Rebibamus!

4. *Roundelay*

1.

Fancy while sitting here
We're in conference
Yet glad in every sense,
Giving no offense,
But joyfully,
Playfully
Singing a round!

2.

Brimful fill the glasses!
Let our hearts beat gladly,
And never fretting sadly,
Cheering ever madly
And joyfully,
Playfully
Sing us a round!

3.

May the noble Virgin,
God's own chosen prize,
The fairest to all eyes,
Rose of paradise,
Be merciful
To drinking folk
Where they may be!

4.

Comrades, let us drink,
Let's enjoy the food
And live in blithesome mood.
Drinking thus is good.
And copiously,
In jollity
Drink ever more!

5.

Hospitem laudemus,
Sibi decantemus
Tunc iterum potemus,
Secundum convivemus,
Honeste,
Modeste
Iubilemus!

5. Olim lacus colueram

1.

Olim lacus colueram,
Olim pulcher exstiteram,
Dum cignus ego fueram.
Miser, Miser!
    Modo niger
    Et ustus fortiter.

2.

Eram nive candidior,
Quavis ave formosior,
Modo sum corvo nigrior.
Miser, miser!
    Modo niger
    Et ustus fortiter!

3.

Me rogus urit fortiter,
Girat, regirat garcifer,
Propinat me nunc dapifer.
Miser, miser!
    Modo niger
    Et ustus fortiter!

5.
Hosteler, we praise you!
Sing to him in chorus,
Then down the drink before us,
Festiveness reign o'er us
And honorably
And decorously
Jubilating!

5. *Song of the Roasted Swan*

1.
I once could call the lake my own,
Where once in stateliness I shone
The while I as a swan was known.
Wretched, wretched!
   Now I'm blackened,
   Roasted to a crisp.

2.
Far whiter was I than the snow,
More fair than any bird I know,
But now I'm blacker than a crow.
Wretched, wretched!
   Now I'm blackened,
   Roasted to a crisp.

3.
The fire ablaze and crackling burns me,
The baster sets me right and turns me,
When butlers serve, no feaster spurns me.
Wretched, wretched!
   Now I'm blackened,
   Roasted to a crisp.

4.
Mallem in aquis vivere,
Nudo semper sub aere,
Quam in hoc mergi pipere.
Miser, miser!
　Modo niger
　Et ustus fortiter!

5.
Nunc in scutella iaceo
Et volitare nequeo,
Dentes frendentes video.
Miser, miser!
　Modo niger
　Et ustus fortiter!

4.

I'd rather to the lake repair
And always breathe the open air
Than all this spice and pepper bear.
Wretched, wretched!
 Now I'm blackened,
 Roasted to a crisp.

5.

Alas, now in the dish I lie
And am no longer fit to fly;
The feasters' gnashing teeth hear I.
Wretched, wretched!
 Now I'm blackened,
 Roasted to a crisp.

CHAPTER III

Songs of Spring and Love

THE FIRST TWO POEMS in this chapter (by far the longest in the collection) are probably of very early date, perhaps from the tenth century. Both are found in the Cambridge songs (see Introduction pp. 14 and 37), the first as No. 41, the second as No. 27. The former, sung by a nun, has been called "a jewel of awakening medieval lyric poetry" by the German critic Paul von Winterfeld. It is of French origin. One is reminded by it of a German love ditty, also apparently by a nun and dating from the twelfth century, which begins: "Thou art mine, I am thine . . . " (*Du bist mîn, ich bin dîn . . .*). Poem 2, also a love song but of a more formal kind, is probably of more recent date.

The rest of these songs, mostly taken from the *Carmina Burana* and dating from the late twelfth and early thirteenth centuries, express the joy of love coupled with the enthusiasm engendered by the coming of the warmer season of the year after a long, bitter northern winter. Some are conventional; some reveal marked similarities in their imagery to the songs of the French troubadours and the German minnesingers. Others again, like poem 7, find a new approach to the general theme of love and achieve striking effects. The love described here does not always lead to happiness (poems 13 and 14); it even prompts the lover to inveigh bitterly against the goddess who is responsible for it (poem 18); and warns the swain that it is stronger than the lure of books and studies (poems 19 and 20).

1. Levis exsurgit zephirus

1.

Levis exsurgit zephirus
et sol procedit tepidus,
iam terra sinus aperit,
dulcore suo diffluit.

2.

Ver purpuratum exiit,
ornatus suos induit,
aspergit terram floribus,
ligna silvarum frondibus.

3.

Struunt lustra quadrupedes
et dulces nidos volucres,
inter ligna florentia
sua decantant gaudia.

4.

Quod oculis dum video
et auribus dum audio,
heu pro tantis gaudiis
tantis inflor suspiriis.

5.

Cum mihi sola sedeo
et hec revolvens palleo,
si forte capud sublevo,
nec audio nec video.

6.

Tu saltim, Veris gratia,
exaudi et considera
frondes, flores et gramina,
nam mea languet anima.

1. *A Maiden's Sighs in Springtime*

1.

The gentle west wind softly blows,
The tepid, warming sunlight glows,
The earth its bosom has revealed,
Its fragrance spread o'er wood and field.

2.

Springtime has come forth many-hued,
Her finery she has indued,
She dots the earth with all her flowers
And fills the wood with leafy bowers.

3.

Four-footed beasts prepare their lairs
And birds build cozy nests in pairs,
In forests green with vegetation
Birds chirp their songs in exultation.

4.

When to my eyes this joy appears,
And when I hear it with my ears,
O then alas for so much pleasure
I must sigh beyond all measure.

5.

When by myself I sit alone
And in reflexion pale have grown,
Perchance I raise my head a bit
But neither hear nor see a whit.

6.

O grace of spring descend on me
I pray, give ear at least and see
The flowers, grasses and the leaves!
For my heart languishes and grieves.

2. Iam, dulcis amica, venito

1.

Iam, dulcis amica, venito,
quam sicut cor meum diligo;
intra in cubiculum meum
ornamentis cunctis ornatum!

2.

Ibi sunt sedilia strata
atque velis domus parata
floresque in domo sparguntur
herbeque fragrantes miscentur.

3.

Est ibi mensa apposita
universis cibis honusta,
ibi clarum vinum habundat
et quicquid te, cara, delectat.

4.

Ibi sonant dulces simphonie
inflantur et altius tibie,
ibi puer et docta puella
canunt tibi cantica pulchra.

5.

Hic cum plectro citharam tangit,
illa melos cum lira pangit
portantque ministri pateras
diversis poculis plenas.

6.

"Ego fui sola in silva
et dilexi loca secreta
fugique frequentius turbam
atque . . . plebis catervam.

7.

. . . .

2. Invitation to the Beloved

1.

My sweetheart, O come to me here,
You, like my own heart, I revere;
Come into my chamber, I pray,
Decked out in a festive array!

2.

There are chairs here for you and for me
And a household of fine tapestry,
And flowers all over the room,
And herbs with their fragrant perfume.

3.

There's a table here laden with food,
All kinds of it, wholesome and good,
There's wine too, it's pure and it's clear,
And whatever pleases you, dear.

4.

What melodies sweet there abound,
Much higher the flutes seem to sound!
Accomplished, both maiden and lad
Sing chanteys dulcet and glad.

5.

With plectrum the zither he plays,
She sings to the lyre her lays,
While bowls the servants bring up
With many an o'erflowing cup.

6.

"Alone I was there in the wood,
Enjoying its cool solitude,
From crowds I have learned how to flee
And . . . mobs disorderly.

7.

. . . .*

*Strophe 7 is textually corrupt.

8.

Non me iuvat tantum convivium,
quantum predulce colloquium,
nec rerum tantarum ubertas
ut cara familiaritas."

9.

Quid iuvat differre, electa,
que sunt tamen post facienda!
Fac cita, quod eris factura,
in me non est aliqua mora.

10.

Iam nunc veni, soror electa
ac omnibus . . . dilecta,
lux mee clara pupille
parsque maior anime mee.

3. Solis iubar nituit

1.

Solis iubar nituit
Nuncians in mundum,
Quod nobis emicuit
Tempus letabundum.
Ver, quod nunc apparuit,
Dans solum fecundum
Salutari meruit
Per carmen iocundum.
    Ergo nostra concio
    Psallat cum tripudio
    Dulci melodia!

8.

To me such a feast is a bore,
I favor a love-gossip more,
I'm cool to a mere plenitude,
But a tête-à-tête, ah, that's good."

9.

't is useless, my dear, to postpone
What none the less has to be done!
Whate'er you'd do, do today,
For I, darling, will not delay.

10.

Come, sweetest, to you hear me call,
To you, loved by one and by all,
You're the light of my eye and a part—
The far better part—of my heart.

3. *To Springtime*

1.

Sun has beamed her brilliant rays,
Telling maid and swain
That for us the happy days
Have returned again.
Springtime has at last appeared,
Fertile is the ground,
Springtime's coming should be cheered
With a jolly round.
  Therefore let our gathering,
  While we dance the three-step, sing
  Dulcet melodies.

2.

Fugiente penitus
Hyemis algore
Spirat ether tacitus
Estu graciore.
Descendente celitus
Salutari rore
Fecundatur funditus
Tellus ex humore.
    Ergo nostra concio
    Psallat cum tripudio
    Dulci melodia!

3.

Sol extinctus fuerat,
Modo renitescit;
Prius invaluerat,
Sed modo tabescit
Nix, que nos obruerat,
Ex estu liquescit;
Qui prius aruerat,
Campus revirescit.
    Ergo nostra concio
    Psallat cum tripudio
    Dulci melodia!

4.

Filomena stridula
Voce modulatur,
Floridum alaudula
Tempus salutatur.
Anus, licet vetula,
Mire petulatur;
Lascivit iuvencula,
Cum sic recreatur.
    Ergo nostra concio
    Psallat cum tripudio
    Dulci melodia!

2.

Since the winter's icy blast
Now has left no trace,
Skies serene have come at last
With a warmer grace.
Dew from heaven now descends,
Wielding blissful power,
With fertility it mends
Earth and field and flower.
   Therefore let our gathering,
   While we dance the three-step, sing
   Dulcet melodies.

3.

Sun has long been out of sight,
Now in strength she grows,
Vanished in their towering height
Are the winter's snows
That have held us long concealed,
Melted now and gone!
See, new life comes o'er the field
That was bare and wan.
   Therefore let our gathering,
   While we dance the three-step, sing
   Dulcet melodies.

4.

See the nightingale, she whirs,
Sings with all her powers,
While the lark herself bestirs,
Greeting spring and flowers.
That old woman—she's a hag—,
How surprising, dances,
While our young and comely Mag,
Sparked by springtime, prances.
   Therefore let our gathering,
   While we dance the three-step, sing
   Dulcet melodies.

4. Letabundus rediit

1.

Letabundus rediit
Avium concentus,
Ver iocundum prodiit—
Gaudeat iuventus
Nova ferens gaudia!
Modo vernant omnia,
Phebus serenatur,
Redolens temperiem
Novo flore faciem
Flora renovatur.

2.

Risu Iovis pellitur
Torpor iemalis,
Alcius extollitur
Cursus estivalis
Solis, beneficio
Cuius omnis regio
Recipit teporem.
Sic ad instar temporis
Nostri Venus pectoris
Reficit ardorem.

3.

Estivantur Driades
Colle sub umbroso,
Prodeunt Oreades
Cetu glorioso,
Satirorum concio
Psallit cum tripudio
Tempe per amena;
His alludens concinit,
Cum iocundi meminit
Veris, Filomena.

4. The Coming of Spring

1.

Birds have come again in swarms,
Happy in their play,
Spring returns with all its charms—
Let young folk be gay
While new pastimes grace the scene!
Tree and bush are turning green,
Phoebus vaunts his powers,
Now, of springtime redolent,
With new blossoms' fragrant scent
Flora sports her flowers.

2.

'neath the smiling face of Jove
Winter's torpor dies,
While to higher heights above
Summer's sunbeams rise,
Through her powers that are legion
Every spot in every region
Feels her warmth anew.
Thus in keeping with the season
Venus has with special reason
Warmed our heartstrings too.

3.

Summering, the Dryads sport
In a shady cove,
Oreads at play cavort,
What a glorious drove!
Many Satyrs, gathering,
Dance the three-step in a ring
Down the lovely vale;
Joining them in merriment,
Celebrating spring's advent
Sings the nightingale.

4.

Estas ab exilio
Redit exoptata,
Picto ridet gremio
Tellus purpurata.
Miti cum susurrio
Suo domicilio
Grillus delectatur.
Hoc canore, iubilo,
Multiformi sibilo
Nemus gloriatur.

5.

Applaudamus igitur
Rerum novitati!
Felix, qui diligitur
Voti compos grati,
Dono letus Veneris,
Cuius ara teneris
Floribus odorat,
Miser e contrario,
Qui sublato bravio
Sine spe laborat!

5. Ecce gratum

1.

Ecce gratum
Et optatum
Ver reducit gaudia,
Purpuratum
Floret pratum,
Sol serenat omnia.
Iam iam cedant tristia!
Estas redit,
Nunc recedit
Hyemis sevicia.

4.

Once the summer took to flight,
Now 't is welcomed back;
With their carpets fresh and bright
Meads no colors lack.
Chirping in their gentle style
From a modest domicile
Crickets sing an earful.
Through their song, their exultation,
Through their varied sibilation
All the grove is cheerful.

5.

Let's applaud, then, and approve
This rejuvenation!
Happy he who's met true love,
Joyful delectation,
Pleased with gifts by Venus lent;
Venus' altar bears the scent
Of flowers' tenderness.
Wretched though that dismal horde
Who bereft of high reward
Toil in hopelessness!

5. *Joys of Springtime*

1.

Spring we've yearned for,
Spring we've burned for,
Spring enlivens all the scene,
Tinged with purple, crimson-hued
Meads with flowers are imbued,
Sun makes everything serene.
Let all sadness come to nought!
Spring has neared—
Disappeared
All the harshness winter brought.

111

2.

Iam liquescit
Et decrescit
Grando, nix et cetera;
Bruma fugit,
Et iam sugit
Veris tellus ubera.
Illi mens est misera,
Qui nec vivit
Nec lascivit
Sub estatis dextera.

3.

Gloriantur
Et letantur
In melle dulcedinis,
Qui conantur,
Ut utantur
Premio Cupidinis.
Simus iussu Cypridis
Gloriantes
Et letantes
Pares esse Paridis!

6. Ver redit optatum

1.

Ver redit optatum
Cum gaudio,
Flore decoratum
Purpureo.
Aves edunt cantus
Quam dulciter.
Revirescit nemus,
Campus est amenus
Totaliter.

2.

See, they've vanished,
See, they're banished,
Hail and snow and all the rest;
Winter's spent,
Spring has lent
Earth its sweetly flowing breast.
He is of a wretched brand
Who'll not gambol,
Lithely amble,
Led by springtime's vernal hand.

3.

Half delirious,
Never serious,
Through the air their singing drifts—
Who aspire
They acquire
Cupid's fascinating gifts.
Venus tells us what to do:
Half delirious,
Never serious,
Let us be like Paris too!

6. *Advice in Spring*

1.

Spring comes, yearned-for spring
With joyful powers,
On his brow a ring
Of crimson flowers.
Birds their song recite,
How sweet the pleasure.
Groves in green are dight,
Fields are our delight
In fullest measure.

2.

Iuvenes, ut flores
Accipiant
Et se per odores
Reficiant,
Virgines assumant
Alacriter
Et eant in prata
Floribus ornata
Communiter!

7. Dum Diane vitrea

1.

Dum Diane vitrea
Sero lampas oritur
Et a fratris rosea
Luce dum succenditur,
Dulcis aura zephyri
Spirans omnes etheri.
Nubes tollit;
Sic emollit
Vis chordarum pectora
Et immutat
Cor, quod nutat
Ad amoris pondera.

2.

Letum iubar Hesperi
Gratiorem
Dat humorem
Roris soporiferi
Mortalium generi.

3.

O quam felix est antidotum soporis,
Quod curarum tempestates sedat et doloris!
Dum surrepit clausis oculorum poris,
Ipsum gaudio equiperat dulcedini amoris.

2.

Youth shall gather flowers
To heart's content,
Take them to their bowers,
Enjoy the scent,
Show, to find a maid,
Alacrity,
Then to meads repair,
Flowers amid their hair
Communally.

7. *Sleep and Love*

1.

When Diana's lamp ascends,
Rising late in silvery sheen,
Till her brother's rosy light
Adds its brightness to the scene;
Then the west wind's softness rare
Mingles with the ethereal air;
     Clouds depart,
     Many a heart
Opens when we hear the lyre,
     Then reviving,
     Newly striving
Love with ardor to inspire.

2.

Hesperus, bright evening star,
     Bathes with dew
     Me and you,
Lulling quietly to sleep
Mortals living near and far.

3.

O how blessèd is such an antidote of sleep,
Stilling storms of worriment, seas of troubles deep!
Stealing through the doors of the eyelid's pores,
Equalling in perfect bliss the lovers' sweetest happiness.

4.

Morpheus in mentem
Trahit impellentem
Ventum lenem segetes maturas,
Murmura rivorum per harenas puras,
Circulares ambitus molendinorum,
Qui furantur somno lumen oculorum.

8. Veris dulcis in tempore

1.

Veris dulcis in tempore
Florenti stat sub arbore
Iuliana cum sorore.
Dulcis amor!
 Qui te caret hoc tempore,
 Fit vilior.

2.

Ecce florescunt arbores,
Lascive canunt volucres,
Inde tepescunt virgines.
Dulcis amor!
 Qui te caret hoc tempore,
 Fit vilior.

3.

Ecce florescunt lilia,
Et virgines dant gemina
Summo deorum carmina.
Dulcis amor!
 Qui te caret hoc tempore,
 Fit vilior.

4.

Si tenerem, quam cupio,
In nemore sub folio,
Oscularer cum gaudio.
Dulcis amor!
 Qui te caret hoc tempore,
 Fit vilior.

4.

Morpheus sends the mind
Gentle gusts of wind,
Wafting breezes kind through ripened grain;
Streams that murmur low o'er the sandy plain,
Mill wheels turning slow, circling day and night—
These rob eyes of light, offering sleep for sight.

8. Song of Love

1.

In the spring—a happy time—
Underneath a blooming lime
Julie with her sister stands.
Ah, that love!
  Whoso now is robbed of thee,
  Wretch is he.

2.

See the blossoms on the tree,
'mongst them birds sing joyfully,
Hearing it, the maidens glow.
Ah, that love!
  Whoso now is robbed of thee,
  Wretch is he.

3.

See the lilies now in flower
And the singing maids that shower
Praises on the god of gods.
Ah, that love!
  Whoso now is robbed of thee,
  Wretch is he.

4.

Were my loved one now beside me
In the grove where green leaves hide me,
I would kiss her fervently.
Ah, that love!
  Whoso now is robbed of thee,
  Wretch is he.

9. Iove cum Mercurio

1.

Iove cum Mercurio
Geminos tenente
Et a Libra Venere
Martem expellente
Virgo nostra nascitur
Tauro tunc latente.

2.

Natus ego pariter
Sub eisdem signis
Pari par coniunctus sum
Legibus benignis,
Paribus est ignibus
Par accensus ignis.

3.

Solus solam diligo,
Sic me sola solum,
Nec est, cui liceat
Immiscere dolum;
Non in vanum variant
Signa nostra polum.

4.

Obicit "ab alio"
Forsitan "amatur,"
Ut, quod "solus" dixerim,
Ita refellatur;
Sed ut dictum maneat,
Sic determinatur.

9. *Bond of Love*

1.

Once when Jove and Mercury
Met to be a twain,
When from Libra Venus freed
Planet Mars amain,
Then our Virgin's birth took place,
But of Taurus—not a trace.

2.

Similarly I was born
Under signs like these,
Equal, I'm to equal joined,
What good auspices!
One twin fire will burn the higher
Kindled by its matching fire.

3.

I alone love her alone,
She loves me, none other,
This our love let no one dare
With deceit to smother.
Our star will not be deflected
Nor to orbits false directed.

4.

Some may say: "Another man
Loves her, I can prove it,"
May refute what I have claimed,
Yes, and may disprove it.
No, let stand what I have stated,
So it is and so 't is fated.

10. Amor habet superos

1.

Amor habet superos,
Iovem amat Iuno,
Motus premens efferos
Imperat Neptuno,
Pluto tenens inferos
Mitis est hoc uno.
   Amoris solamine
   Virgino cum virgine,
   Aro non in semine,
   Pecco sine crimine.

2.

Amor trahit teneros
Molliori nexu,
Rigidos et asperos
Duro frangit flexu,
Capitur rinosceros
Virginis amplexu.
   Amoris solamine
   Virgino cum virgine,
   Aro non in semine,
   Pecco sine crimine.

3.

Virgo cum virginibus
Horreo corruptas
Et cum meretricibus
Simul odi nuptas,
Nam in istis talibus
Turpis est voluptas.
   Amoris solamine
   Virgino cum virgine,
   Aro non in semine,
   Pecco sine crimine.

10. Cecilia

1.

Love controls the gods on high,
Juno loves her Jove,
When untamed love's passions fly,
Neptune too must love,
Pluto of the lower throne
Favors love and love alone.
  Needing solace, care beladen,
  I go flirting with a maiden,
  Where I've plowed no seeds go in,
  I don't wrong though I may sin.

2.

Love draws in the tender souls
With a gentle band,
Twists the mulish ones with holds
That they scarce can stand.
Rhinos too succumb to charms
When they're in a maiden's arms.
  Needing solace, care beladen,
  I go flirting with a maiden,
  Where I've plowed no seeds go in,
  I don't wrong though I may sin.

3.

How I love a maid demure,
Yet I've never tarried
With a girl that is not pure,
Nor with one that's married.
For with such in every case
Pleasure turns to something base.
  Needing solace, care beladen,
  I go flirting with a maiden,
  Where I've plowed no seeds go in,
  I don't wrong though I may sin.

4.

Virginis egregie
Ignibus calesco
Et eius cotidie
In amore cresco;
Sol est in meridie,
Nec ego tepesco.
  Amoris solamine
  Virgino cum virgine,
  Aro non in semine,
  Pecco sine crimine.

5.

Gratus super omnia
Ludus est puelle,
Et eius precordia
Omni carent felle;
Sunt, que prestat, basia
Dulciora melle.
  Amoris solamine
  Virgino cum virgine,
  Aro non in semine,
  Pecco sine crimine.

6.

Ludo cum Cecilia—
Nichil timeatis!
Sum quasi custodia
Fragilis etatis,
Ne marcescant lilia
Sue castitatis.
  Amoris solamine
  Virgino cum virgine,
  Aro non in semine,
  Pecco sine crimine.

4.

Heated in a maiden's fire,
Ardently I glow,
In her passion rising higher
My love too will grow,
Though the noonday sun may flame,
I will still remain the same.
  Needing solace, care beladen,
  I go flirting with a maiden,
  Where I've plowed no seeds go in,
  I don't wrong though I may sin.

5.

Nothing could exceed my fun
Flirting with a lass,
So her heart will always shun
Gall and manners crass;
While her kisses, I declare,
Are as sweet as honeyed fare.
  Needing solace, care beladen,
  I go flirting with a maiden,
  Where I've plowed no seeds go in,
  I don't wrong though I may sin.

6.

With Cecilia I sport—
Still, allay your fears!
I shall guard the open fort,
Shield her tender years
Lest her chastity feel anguish,
Lest its pure white lilies languish.
  Needing solace, care beladen,
  I go flirting with a maiden,
  Where I've plowed no seeds go in,
  I don't wrong though I may sin.

7.

Flos est, florem frangere
Non est res secura.
Uvam sino crescere,
Donec sit matura;
Spes me facit vivere
Letum re ventura.
  Amoris solamine
  Virgino cum virgine,
  Aro non in semine,
  Pecco sine crimine.

8.

Volo tantum ludere,
Id est contemplari,
Presens loqui, tangere,
Tandem osculari.
Quintum, quod est agere,
Noli suspicari!
  Amoris solamine
  Virgino cum virgine,
  Aro non in semine,
  Pecco sine crimine.

9.

Quicquid agant ceteri,
Virgo, sic agamus,
Ut, quem decet fieri,
Ludum faciamus—
Ambo sumus teneri,
Tenere ludamus!
  Amoris solamine
  Virgino cum virgine,
  Aro non in semine,
  Pecco sine crimine.

7.

She's a flower one must not rape,
That I would abjure,
Never will I touch the grape
Till it is mature;
Hope will let me live to see
What the future holds for me.
   Needing solace, care beladen,
   I go flirting with a maiden,
   Where I've plowed no seeds go in,
   I don't wrong though I may sin.

8.

I would have a mere flirtation,
Make eyes at the miss,
Stroke her while in conversation,
Lastly take a kiss.
But the fifth step—action? No!
Think not that so far I'd go.
   Needing solace, care beladen,
   I go flirting with a maiden,
   Where I've plowed no seeds go in,
   I don't wrong though I may sin.

9.

Others' deeds are not for us,
Maiden, let us play
Only what is decorous,
Seek a seemly way—
We are both in tender youth,
Let our games be not uncouth.
   Needing solace, care beladen,
   I go flirting with a maiden,
   Where I've plowed no seeds go in,
   I don't wrong though I may sin.

11. Lingua mendax et dolosa

1.

Lingua mendax et dolosa,
Lingua procax, venenosa,
Lingua digna detruncari
Et in igne concremari,

2.

Que me dicit deceptorem
Et non fidum amatorem,
Quam amabam, dimisisse
Et ad alteram transisse.

3.

Sciat deus, sciant dei:
Non sum reus huius rei.
Sciant dei, sciat deus:
Huius rei non sum reus.

4.

Unde iuro Musas novem,
Quod et maius est, per Iovem,
Qui pro Dane sumpsit auri,
In Europa formam tauri.

5.

Iuro Phebum, iuro Martem,
Qui amoris sciant artem,
Iuro quoque te, Cupido,
Arcum cuius reformido.

6.

Arcum iuro cum sagittis,
Quas frequenter in me mittis:
Sine fraude, sine dolo
Fedus hoc servare volo.

7.

Volo fedus observare
Et ad hec dicemus, quare:
Inter choros puellarum
Nichil vidi tam preclarum.

11. *Pledge of Love*

1.

Lying tongue and false with slander,
Poison tongue that stirs my dander,
Tongue that should be separated
From the throat, to be cremated,

2.

Tongue that called me a deceiver,
Faithless me who'd up and leave her,
Whom I loved and then dismissed,
Going to another tryst.

3.

Hear it, god, hear, gods transcendent:
I'm an innocent defendant,
Hear ye gods, hear god on high,
Guiltless of such crime am I.

4.

By the Muses nine I swear,
Better still, by Jupiter,
Who for Danae turned to gold,
For Europa to a steer, I'm told.

5.

Mars I swear by and Apollo—
Arts of love are theirs to follow—
Cupid by you too I swear,
Though your bow is my despair.

6.

By your bow, I swear, and arrow
That oft penetrates my marrow:
Shunning fraud or falsity,
Sacred is this pledge to me.

7.

From this pledge I will not shy,
And I'll tell the reason why:
I've encountered many a girl,
Never such a precious pearl.

8.

Inter quas appares ita
Ut in auro margarita.
Humeri, pectus et venter
Sunt formata tam decenter.

9.

Frons et gula, labra, mentum
Dant amoris alimentum;
Crines eius adamavi,
Quoniam fuere flavi.

10.

Ergo dum nox erit dies
Et dum labor erit quies
Et dum aqua erit ignis
Et dum silva sine lignis

11.

Et dum mare sine velis
Et dum Partus sine telis,
Cara michi semper eris:
Nisi fallar, non falleris.

12. De pollicito

1.

De pollicito
Mea mens elata
In proposito
Vivit, animata
Spei merito;
Tamen dubito,
Ne spes alterata
Cedat subito.

8.

You are cast in finer mold,
Like a pearl that's set in gold.
Yea, in shoulders, waist and breast
You are fairer than the rest.

9.

Neck and lips and chin and forehead
Make my love for you more torrid;
Fair her tresses make me fond,
They're so radiantly blond.

10.

So till night turns into day,
Labor into rest and play,
Water flames as fiery seas,
Woodlands are in want of trees,

11.

Till the sea no sails can show,
Till the Parthian lacks his bow,
Always will I love but you,
Never fail you if you're true.

12. *Love's Sorrow*

1.

Through her promise given
All my spirit burns,
Hearing her intent
It is raised to heaven
With a newborn hope;
Yet my doubt returns,
Fears my hope will be
Shattered suddenly.

2.

"Uni faveo,
Uni, dico, stelle,
Cuius roseo
Basia cum melle
Stillant oleo.
In hac rideo,
In ipsius velle
Totus ardeo."

3.

Amor nimius
Incutit timorem,
Timor anxius
Suscitat ardorem
Vehemencius,
Ita dubius
Sencio dolorem
Certo cercius.

4.

"Totus Veneris
Uror in camino;
Donis Cereris,
Saciatis vino
Presto ceteris
Et cum superis
Nectare divino
Fruor prosperis."

13. Dulce solum

1.

Dulce solum
Natalis patrie,
Domus ioci,
Thalamus gracie,
Vos relinquam
Aut cras aut hodie,
Periturus
Amoris rabie.

2.

One girl I adore,
One, my star, I say,
Lips adrip with honey
Stored by bees in May,
Drip with balsam too.
When I smile her way,
Noting her desire,
I am all on fire.

3.

Love that asks too much
Causes fear and anguish,
Fear that's all too anxious
Has an ardent touch,
Is impetuous,
Making lovers languish;
Grief and doubt are sure,
Nothing could be truer.

4.

Being all aflame
With Dame Venus' fire,
Ceres' gifts and wine
Let me never claim,
Leaving them to others.
Higher's my desire,
With the gods I'll sup
Nectar from my cup.

13. *Deadly Love*

1.

You, sweetest soil,
O land of my birth,
Homeland of jest,
Chamber of mirth,
You I will leave
Now or tomorrow,
Destined to die
Of Love's deep sorrow.

2.

Vale tellus,
Valete socii,
Quos benigno
Favore colui,
Et me dulcis
Consortem studii
Deplangite,
Qui vobis perii!

3.

Igne novo
Veneris saucia
Mens, que prius
Non novit talia,
Nunc fatetur
Vera proverbia:
"Ubi amor,
Ibi miseria."

4.

Quot sunt apes
In Yble vallibus,
Quot vestitur
Dodona frondibus
Et quot natant
Pisces equoribus,
Tot abundat
Amor doloribus.

14. Huc usque me miseram

1.

Huc usque me miseram,
Rem bene celaveram
Et amavi callide.

2.

Res mea tandem patuit,
Nam venter intumuit,
Partus instat gravide.

2.

Sweet land, farewell,
O comrades, adieu,
Kindly regards
Attach me to you,
Mourn for me,
You whom I cherished,
Allies in my studies—
Lost to you, perished!

3.

New fire of Venus
Wounded my heart,
Never I've suffered
So grievous a smart.
Proverbs are saying
What is too true:
Where there is love
There's misery too.

4.

Many as bees
As in Hybla's swale,
Many as leaves
That Dodona veil,
Many as fish
That in oceans live,
So much grief
Cupid can give.

14. *The Deserted Girl*

1.

Up to now, ah wretched me,
I could hide it skillfully,
Crafty was my love-affair.

2.

Yet at last the people knew,
For my belly grew and grew,
Soon a child I'd have to bear.

3.
Hinc mater me verberat,
Hinc pater improperat,
Ambo tractant aspere.

4.
Sola domi sedeo,
Egredi non audeo
Nec inpalam ludere.

5.
Cum foris egredior,
A cunctis inspicior,
Quasi monstrum fuerim.

6.
Cum vident hunc uterum,
Alter pulsat alterum,
Silent, dum transierim.

7.
Semper pulsant cubito,
Me designant digito,
Ac si mirum fecerim.

8.
Nutibus me indicant,
Dignam rogo iudicant,
Quod semel peccaverim.

9.
Quid percurram singula?
Ego sum in fabula
Et in ore omnium.

10.
Ex eo vim pacior,
Iam dolore morior,
Semper sum in lacrimis.

11.
Hoc dolorem cumulat,
Quod amicus exulat
Propter illud paululum.

3.

How for this my mother beats me,
To abuse my father treats me!
Badly at their hands I fare.

4.

All alone I sit at home,
Never do I dare to roam,
Nor to breathe the open air.

5.

When I go to take a walk
Everybody stops to gawk,
Just as though a monster passed.

6.

When they see this bulging belly,
Bill will stare and nudge his Nelly,
Silent till I'm gone at last.

7.

Elbows poke their neighbor's side,
Pointing fingers that would chide,
At this miracle aghast.

8.

When I come, a sign they make
That I'm worthy of the stake,
Though but once I sinned, poor lass.

9.

Why should I rehearse all that?
I'm in every chit and chat,
Tongues I spur that thrive on patter.

10.

That's why I am close to madness,
Why I'm almost dead of sadness,
Weeping nearly all the time.

11.

Deepest sorrow has assailed me
Since the one I love has failed me
For this trifling little matter.

12.

Ob patris seviciam
Recessit in Franciam
A finibus ultimis.

13.

Sum iam in tristicia
De eius absencia
In doloris cumulum.

15. Volo virum vivere

1.

Volo virum vivere
Viriliter,
Diligam, si diligar
Equaliter;
Sic amandum censeo,
Non aliter.
Hac in parte forcior
Quam Iupiter
Nescio procari
Commercio vulgari,
Amaturus forsitan
Volo prius amari.

2.

Muliebris animi
Superbiam
Gravi supercilio
Despiciam
Nec maiorem terminum
Subiciam
Neque bubus aratrum
Preficiam.
Displicet hic usus
In miseros diffusus,
Malo plaudens ludere
Quam plangere delusus.

12.

Ah, my dad was too severe,
Gone to France is now my dear,
Far away in a distant clime.

13.

Sad am I and all alone
Now my dearest love is gone,
Gnawing grief has left me shattered.

15. *The Man's Wish*

1.

As a man I like to live—
And virilely.
I will love if I am loved—
And equally;
Thus I think that love should be
Not different, sir.
Stronger I in this regard
Than Jupiter,
I can't sue nor pray
In a base commercial way,
For if I'm perchance to love
The girl must love me first.

2.

When I find a woman's mind
With haughty ways,
Condescendingly indeed
On her I gaze.
Nothing that is higher placed
Would I debase,
Nor the plow before the ox
I'd want to place,
Holding in deep despite
The ways of a wretched wight:
Sooner frolic with applause
Than jilted mourn my plight.

3.

Que cupit, ut placeat,
Huic placeam;
Ipsa prior faveat,
Ut faveam.
Non ludemus aliter
Hanc aleam,
Ne se granum reputet,
Me paleam.
Pari lege fori
Deserviam amori,
Ne prosternar impudens
Femineo pudori.

4.

Liber ego liberum
Me iactito,
Casto pene similis
Hippolyto,
Nec me vincit mulier
Tam subito.
Que seducat, oculis
Ac digito
Dicat me placere
Et diligat sincere;
Hec michi protervitas
Placet in muliere.

5.

Ecce michi displicet,
Quod cecini,
Et meo contrarius
Sum carmini,
Tue reus, domina,
Dulcedini,
Cuius elegancie
Non memini.
Quia sic erravi,
Sum dignus pena gravi;
Penitentem corripe,
Si placet, in conclavi!

3.

If she wants to please the man,
I'll help her to it,
She must show me favor first,
Then I will do it.
So to play our game of dice
O let us try.
Shun the thought that she's the grain,
While chaff am I.
Just one rule have we?
A lover then I'll be!
I'd not bow barefacedly
Before her prudishness.

4.

I am free and call me so
Without a fuss,
Almost like that hero chaste
Hippolytus.
Conquer me no woman will
In a sudden wise.
If she'd win with finger raised
And sparkling eyes,
Say I please her really
With love for me sincerely;
Such a maner pert and bold
In her I'd fain behold.

5.

Stop, this song displeases me
That I've recited,
My opinion contradicts
What I've indited.
To your sweetness, lady mine,
I've wrought a harm,
For I failed to give a thought
To all your charm.
Since on error bent
I've earned grave punishment.
Please, O seize the penitent
And lock him in your chamber.

16. Grates ago Veneri

1a.

Grates ago Veneri,
Que prosperi
Michi risus numine
De virgine
Mea gratum
Et optatum
Contulit tropheum.

1b.

Dudum militaveram
Nec poteram
Hoc frui stipendio;
Nunc sencio
Me beari,
Serenari
Vultum Dioneum.

2a.

Visu, colloquio,
Contactu, basio
Frui virgo dederat,
Sed aberat
Linea posterior
Et melior
Amoris.
Quam nisi transiero,
De cetero
Sunt, que dantur alia,
Materia furoris.

16. Coronis

1a.

Thanks to Venus I convey,
Her smiles today
Kindly, with propitious power,
Gave me this hour
Luck I hoped for,
Luck I groped for
With the girl I love.

1b.

Oft I strove and strove again,
But all in vain,
This reward and prize to earn;
I now discern
Joy's fast pace,
Dione's face
Shows a kindly cast.

2a.

I long could cherish each:
Her glance, her touch and speech,
Also now and then a kiss,
But ah, I miss
That which follows all the rest,
The very best
Love offers.
But if this I must forgo
The rest, I know,
Is not more and is not less
Than what our passion proffers.

2b.

Ad metam propero,
Sed fletu tenero
Mea me sollicitat,
Dum dubitat
Solvere virguncula
Repagula
Pudoris.
Flentis bibo lacrimas
Dulcissimas,
Sic me plus inebrio
Plus haurio fervoris.

3a.

Delibuta lacrimis
Oscula plus sapiunt,
Blandimentis intimis
Mentem plus alliciunt.
Ergo magis capior
Et acrior
Vis flamme recalescit.
Sed dolor Coronidis
Se tumidis
Exerit singultibus
Nec precibus
Mitescit.

3b.

Preces addo precibus
Basiaque basiis,
Fletus illa fletibus,
Iurgia conviciis.
Meque cernit oculo
Nunc emulo,
Nunc quoque supplicanti.
Nam nunc lite dimicat,
Nunc supplicat,
Dumque prece blandior,
Fit surdior
Precanti.

2b.

I haste my goal to reach,
But she, she will beseech.
Tears will flow that scarce abate.
She'll hesitate
Now at last to turn the key
And yield for me
Her maidenhood,
As she weeps, her tears I savor,
How sweet their flavor,
As I drink, the higher rises
My wild impassioned mood.

3a.

Kisses that with tears are wet,
They are kisses quite apart,
With caresses intimate
They entice and lure the heart.
Thus I feel more zest and hunger,
And stronger
The flame will radiate.
But the grief Coronis bears
She sadly airs,
Sighing as though her heart would break.
No pleas could make
Her grief abate.

3b.

Pleas I add to pleading cries,
Kisses adding on to kisses,
Tears with tears she multiplies,
Words of sharp rebuke she hisses.
First she merely seems to eye me
And would deny me,
Then supplicatingly.
For at first she altercates,
Then supplicates.
While I coax and tease, she spurns,
Deaf ears she turns
To every plea.

4a.

Vim nimis audax infero,
Hec ungue sevit aspero,
Comas vellit,
Vim repellit
Strennua,
Sese plicat
Et intricat
Genua,
Ne ianua
Pudoris resolvatur.

4b.

Sed tandem ultra milito,
Triumphum do proposito.
Per amplexus
Firmo nexus,
Bracchia
Eius ligo,
Pressa figo
Basia,
Sic regia
Diones reseratur.

5a.

Res utrique placuit,
Et me minus arguit
Micior amasia
Dans basia
Mellita.

5b.

Et subridens tremulis
Semiclausis oculis
Veluti sub anxio
Suspirio
Sopita.

4a.

Too bold I now grow violent,
She scratches me with angry bent,
Pulls my hair
With strength to spare,
Fights me—the tease—;
Her legs she crosses,
Then she forces
Together her knees,
Lest the wall
Of chastity should fall.

4b.

But on and on I wage the fight
Until my triumph is in sight.
Hugs and sighs
Strengthen our ties.
Both of her arms
Tightly I bind.
Her lips I find,
Sensing her charms,
So Dione's castle
Becomes my ready vassal.

5a.

Now this tussle pleased us both!
Now no longer was she wroth.
In a milder mood was she,
Offering kisses free
Honey sweet.

5b.

As she smiled, with eyelids blinking,
While her glances kept on sinking,
As if anxiously, she sighed,
Her face I spied:
Asleep now!

17. Quam velim virginum

1.

Quam velim virginum,
Si detur opcio,
Consulti pectoris
Utar iudicio.
Non vagam animo,
Non turpem faciam
Thori participem,
Curarum sociam.
   Pudoris prodigam
   Non eligam
   Nec Sabinam moribus
   Amoribus.

2.

Non curo teneram
Etate primula,
Non arat sapiens
In tali vitula.
Est enim sacius
Cognosse puberam,
Que blandam senciat
Ex equo Venerem.

3.

Si ruga lineas
Suas araverit,
Senecta capiti
Nives asperserit;
Non declinaverim
Ad eius gremium,
Licet in purpura
Redimat senium.
   Tam mea, tam meus est
   Deliciosus Amor,
   Deliciosa Venus.

17. *The Love of My Choice*

1.

I will the judgment use
Of one with reason blest
To choose, if choice I have,
The maid that suits me best.
The fickle I detest,
The shameless I decry
As sharer of my bed
And as my soul's ally.
   Excessive chastity
   I always flee,
   Sabine morals I abjure,
   They rout amour.

2.

No tender maid I'll lure,
Girl half and woman half;
Wise men will not take up
With such a little calf.
For better 't is by far
To love one who's mature,
Who feels Dame Venus' charm
As potently as I.

3.

When once my face is lined
And deep with furrows wrinkled,
And age upon my head
Its silvery snow has sprinkled,
To such a maiden's lap
No more I'll be inclined,
Though age redeems itself
With presents purple-lined.
   They both are friends to me:
   Delightful Cupid, he,
   Delightful Venus, she.

18. Invehar in Venerem

1.

Invehar in Venerem,
  Nisi resipiscat
  Et dediscat
Veterem
    Malignandi spiritum,
      Quo principiis
      Blanditur
      Et blandiciis
      Molitur
      Tristem letis exitum.
R. Non est grata satis
  Ni se Venus gratis
    Exibeat;
    Nam si venit, ut veneat,
    Cum debeat
    Beare, magis debeat.

2.

Prius de ludibrio
  Veneris incertus,
  Nunc expertus
Sentio,
    Quam si male fidei;
      Non exaudior
      Blanditus,
      Unde blandior
      Invitus
      Et invitor invehi.
R. Non est grata satis
  Ni se Venus gratis
    Exibeat;
    Nam si venit, ut veneat,
    Cum debeat
    Beare, magis debeat.

18. *Invective against Venus*

1.

Venus 't is that I'd attack
  If she'd show no sense
  Nor dispense
With her old
    Malice and affected air;
      At the very start
        She entices
        Then to flattery's art
        So jolly
      She a sad end would prepare.
R. I'll not bid her stay
  If she hopes for pay
  Whenever she appears;
  For she's more in debt when she
  Exhibits venal leers
  Than when her boons are voluntary.

2.

Venus used to puzzle me,
  For she was a flirt;
  Now I, alert,
Realize
    That I must distrust her ay;
      She ignores my chatter,
        Though I wheedle;
      Therefore I flatter
        Against my will,
      And I'm tempted to inveigh.
R. I'll not bid her stay
  If she hopes for pay
  Whenever she appears;
  For she's more in debt when she
  Exhibits venal leers
  Than when her boons are voluntary.

3.

Ab annis cepi teneris
Cum miseris
Servire castris Veneris
     Nec adhuc statum muto;
Sed cum sim pene penitus
Emeritus,
Adhuc me vexat servitus
     Et adigit tributo.
R. Non est grata satis
Ni se Venus gratis
     Exibeat;
     Nam si venit ut veneat,
Cum debeat
Beare, magis debeat.

4.

In hoc se gessit forcius
Quam alius
Laertis ille filius,
     Cuius caput inmune
Ab hac transit angaria
Sollercia,
Qui solus Solis filia
     Potitus est impune.
R. Non est grata satis
Ni se Venus gratis
     Exibeat;
     Nam si venit, ut veneat,
Cum debeat
Beare, magis debeat.

3.

Because in tender years I started
To serve in Venus'
Detested host, I ne'er departed
  This worship then or now;
So I, without ado or fuss
Emeritus,
Still chafe and fret in servitude
  And tribute to her vow.
R. I'll not bid her stay
  If she hopes for pay
  Whenever she appears;
  For she's more in debt when she
  Exhibits venal leers
  Than when her boons are voluntary.

4.

In boldness not to be outdone
By other men
We find Laertes' famous son,
  Whose head emerged scot-free
From trickish villainage and ruse
That she could use.
This son subdued the sungod's daughter
  With full impunity.
R. I'll not bid her stay
  If she hopes for pay
  Whenever she appears;
  For she's more in debt when she
  Exhibits venal leers
  Than when her boons are voluntary.

5.

Cur amo, si non amor?
Satius est, ut amor
 In odium vertatur.
  Sed absit, quod amantium
  Remedium sit odium,
  Quod initum per gaudium
  Consorcium divorcium
  Per gaudii contrarium
Sorciatur.
R. Non est grata satis
 Ni se Venus gratis
  Exibeat;
  Nam si venit, ut veneat,
  Cum debeat
  Beare, magis debeat.

6.

In odium converti
Nec ius amoris certi
 Nec finis est probandus.
  Amorem enim odio
  Si finio, si vitio
  Per vitum subvenio,
  Desipio, si studio
  Sanitatis insanio
Non sanandus.
R. Non est grata satis
 Ni se Venus gratis
  Exibeat;
  Nam si venit, ut veneat,
  Cum debeat
  Beare, magis debeat.

5.

Should I love if I'm not loved?
Better 't would be that love
    Be turned at once to hate.
        But let it not be lover's fate
        That cure for love be found in hate.
        That unions which, the time they started
        Were happy, end when lovers parted,
        And cause the opposite of gladness—
Deep sadness.
R. I'll not bid her stay
        If she hopes for pay
        Whenever she appears;
        For she's more in debt when she
        Exhibits venal leers
        Than when her boons are voluntary.

6.

To turn to hatred's banner
Is not true lovers' manner,
    No way for love to end.
        For if my love with hate I rend
        And flaws with other flaws would mend,
        I'm foolish, as indeed I'd be
        If, though there is no cure for me,
        I'd lose my mind in search of one—
I'd be undone.
R. I'll not bid her stay
        If she hopes for pay
        Whenever she appears;
        For she's more in debt when she
        Exhibits venal leers
        Than when her boons are voluntary.

19. Omittamus studia

1.

Omittamus studia,
Dulce est desipere,
Et carpamus dulcia
Iuventutis tenere!
Res est apta senectuti
Seriis intendere,
(Res est apta iuventuti
Leta mente ludere).
   Velox etas preterit
   Studio detenta,
   Lascivire suggerit
   Tenera iuventa.

2.

Ver etatis labitur,
Hiems nostra properat,
Vita damnum patitur,
Cura carnem macerat.
Sanguis aret, hebet pectus,
Minuuntur gaudia,
Nos deterret iam senectus
Morborum familia.
   Velox etas preterit
   Studio detenta,
   Lascivire suggerit
   Tenera iuventa.

19. Adieu to Studies

1.

Books and studies we'll omit
With abandon—sweet is play,
To such pleasures let us flit
As entice young men in May!
Aptly is old age resigned
To a serious occupation,
But the young folk often find
Happiness in recreation.
  Time we're wasting speedily
  While to books confined,
  Tender youth suggests that we
  Be to fun inclined.

2.

Soon the spring of life is over,
Winter comes to us in haste,
Life its losses will discover,
Care will make the body waste.
Blood dries up and spirit fails us,
Pleasures shrink and come to naught,
't is old age that now assails us,
With disease and suffering fraught.
  Time we're wasting speedily
  While to books confined,
  Tender youth suggests that we
  Be to fun inclined.

3.

Imitemur superos!
Digna est sentencia,
Et amoris teneros
Iam venantur recia.
Voto nostro serviamus!
Mos est iste numinum.
Ad plateas descendamus
Et choreas virginum!
   Velox etas preterit
   Studio detenta,
   Lascivire suggerit
   Tenera iuventa.

4.

Ibi, que fit facilis,
Est videndi copia,
Ibi fulget mobilis
Membrorum lascivia.
Dum puelle se movendo
Gestibus lasciviunt,
Asto videns, et videndo
Me michi subripiunt.
   Velox etas preterit
   Studio detenta,
   Lascivire suggerit
   Tenera iuventa.

3.
Let us live like gods above!
Worthy is this sentiment,
See, the hunting nets of love
Wait for those on loving bent.
To our vows let us attend!
That is what the custom says.
Let us to the streets descend,
To the maidens' choruses.
    Time we're wasting speedily
    While to books confined,
    Tender youth suggests that we
    Be to fun inclined.

4.
There the watchful lad may see
Which among the maids is best,
There young folk capriciously
Flash through dances breast to breast,
While each girl her arms is raising,
Whirling in a pirouette,
There I stand agape and gazing,
Then myself I quite forget.
    Time we're wasting speedily
    While to books confined,
    Tender youth suggests that we
    Be to fun inclined.

20. Vacillantis trutine

1a.
Vacillantis trutine
Libramine
Mens suspensa fluctuat
Et estuat
In tumultus anxios,
Dum se vertit
Et bipertit
Motus in contrarios.
 O langueo,
 Causam languoris video
 Nec caveo,
 Videns et prudens pereo.
1b.
Me vacare studio
Vult racio;
Sed dum amor alteram
Vult operam,
In diversa rapior.
Racione
Cum Dione
Dimicante crucior.
 O langueo,
 Causam languoris video
 Nec caveo,
 Videns et prudens pereo.

20. *Love and Studies*

1a.

While my heart hung there suspended
Upon the scale,
How it wavered, fluctuated,
So unabated
In its fear tumultuous,
While it tended,
While it bended
In two channels tortuous.
 I languish, Oh,
  The cause of this I clearly know,
  But what care I?
  Seeing and knowing this, I die.

1b.

I should take the time to study,
So reason bids;
But no such activity
Does love decree,
Pointing to a different path.
Reason says so,
Dione says no,
I'm the victim of their wrath.
 I languish, Oh,
  The cause of this I clearly know,
  But what care I?
  Seeing and knowing this, I die.

2a.

Sicut in arbore
Frons tremula,
Navicula
Levis in equore,
Dum caret anchore
Subsidio,
Contrario
Flatu concussa fluitat:
Sic agitat,
Sic turbine sollicitat
Me dubio
Hinc amor, inde racio.
   O langueo,
   Causam languoris video
   Nec caveo,
   Videns et prudens pereo.

2b.

Sub libra pondero,
Quid melius,
Et dubius
Mecum delibero.
Nunc menti refero
Delicias venerias,
Que mea michi Florula
Det oscula,
Qui risus, que labellula,
Que facies,
Frons, naris aut cesaries.
   O langueo,
   Causam languoris video
   Nec caveo,
   Videns et prudens pereo.

2a.

Just as on the tree
The trembling leaf,
A little skiff
Cradles from side to side,
To no achor tied
That keeps it at ease,
While a contrary breeze
Now rocks and bobs it back and forth—,
So I am flayed,
So in each eddy I am swayed
By reason hither,
By love, its adversary, thither.
   I languish, Oh,
     The cause of this I clearly know,
     But what care I?
     Seeing and knowing this, I die.

2b.

I'm in the scale and muse
What is the better,
Then held in doubt
And pensive, I reflect,
Until I recollect
The favors of her tender love
That Florula bestowed on me,
The kisses free,
The smiles, the lips inviting me,
Such features rare,
Such forehead, nose, such lovely hair.
   I languish, Oh,
     The cause of this I clearly know,
     But what care I?
     Seeing and knowing this, I die.

3a.

His invitat
Et irritat
Amor me blandiciis.
Sed aliis
Racio sollicitat
Et excitat
Me studiis.
  O langueo,
  Causam languoris video
  Nec caveo,
  Videns et prudens pereo.

3b.

Nam solari
Me scolari
Cogitat exilio.
Sed, racio,
Procul abi! Vinceris
Sub Veneris imperio.
  O langueo,
  Causam languoris video
  Nec caveo,
  Videns et prudens pereo.

21. Si puer cum puellula

1.

Si puer cum puellula
Moraretur in cellula—
R. Felix coniunctio
Amore succrescente,   pari remedio,
Propulso procul tedio.

2.

Fit ludus ineffabilis
Membris, lacertis, labiis—
R. Felix coniunctio
Amore succrescente,   pari remedio,
Propulso procul tedio.

3a.

Love invites me,
It incites me
To allurements such as these.
But reason shows
Me studies new, new pursuits
With new fruits
That I might seize.
    I languish, Oh,
      The cause of this I clearly know,
    But what care I?
    Seeing and knowing this, I die.

3b.

Reason's planning
To be banning
Me to drain an exile's cup.
O reason, stop!
Go away, you will succumb
And then be under Venus' thumb.
    I languish, Oh,
      The cause of this I clearly know,
    But what care I?
    Seeing and knowing this, I die.

21. *A Sport with Endless Charms*

1.

If Meg should chance to meet with Harry
In any room where both can tarry—
R.   Glad is their reunion
As mutual love increases,   for both one remedy,
    Of tedium completely free.

2.

A sport begins with endless charms
Of limbs, of lips on lips, of arms—
R.   Glad is their reunion
As mutual love increases,   for both one remedy,
    Of tedium completely free.

22. Veni, veni, venias

1.

Veni, veni, venias
Ne me mori facias!
Hyria, hyrie,
Nazaza trillirivos!

2.

Pulchra tibi facies,
Oculorum acies,
Capillorum series—
O quam clara species!

3.

Rosa rubicundior,
Lilio candidior,
Omnibus formosior,
Semper in te glorior!

23. Stetit puella

1.

Stetit puella
Rufa tunica;
Si quis eam tetigit,
Tunica crepuit.
           eia!

2.

Stetit puella
Tamquam rosula:
Facie splenduit
Et os eius floruit.
           eia!

3.

Stetit puella   *bi einem boume,*
scripsit amorem   *an eime loube.*
Dar chom Venus also fram;
Caritatem magnam,
Hohe minne
Bot si ir manne.

22. *A Song of Love*

1.

Come, my dear, come, come, I pray,
Do not make me die today!—
Hyria, hyrie,
Nazaza trillirivos!

2.

Your complexion's smooth as cream,
Pretty are your eyes that gleam,
Lovely the hair in pigtails two,
O how beautiful are you!—

3.

Redder than the roses tender,
Whiter than the lily's splendor,
Ne'er such comeliness I've seen,
Glory to you, beauteous queen!—

23. *Girl in Red Tunic*

1.

There stood a maid
In a tunic red;
Whenever you touched the girl
The tunic gave a swirl.
　　　　　eia!

2.

A maid I could see,
Like a rose was she:
With a countenance rare
And lips so red and fair.
　　　　　eia!

3.

There stood a maid　　beneath a tree,
She scribbled love　　upon a leaf.
Along came Venus on the move;
Great love,
High love
Girl offered lover.

165

1. Estivali sub fervore

1.

Estivali sub fervore,
Quando cuncta sunt in flore,
Totus eram in ardore.
Sub olive me decore,
Estu fessum et sudore,
Detinebat mora.

2.

Erat arbor hec in prato
Quovis flore picturato,
Herba, fonte, situ grato,
Sed et umbra, flatu dato.
Stilo non pinxisset Plato
Loca graciora.

CHAPTER IV

Pastorals

THE VAGABOND PASTORALS, like the French *pastourelles,* fall into a special category of love poetry. Set in a bucolic, Arcadian scene, they are conventional and stylized. But here the Latin vagabond poet succeeds in introducing a more outspoken form of sensualism than is found in later pastoral poetry. The shepherdess may give her consent (poem 2), or she may offer good reasons for rejecting the shepherd's pleas (poem 1). In one case she abandons her resistance when he rescues her sheep from a wolf (poem 4), and in another his superior strength wins the day (poem 3).

All these pastorals may well be of Romance origin.

1. *The Shepherdess Says No*

1.

In the summer's torrid heat,
When the flowers blossom sweet,
All aglow from head to feet
'neath an olive tree I squatted,
By fatigue and sweat besotted,
There to stay a while.

2.

It was in a field where grew
Vivid flowers of every hue,
Grass, a fount with waters blue,
Shade too and a welcome breeze.
More delightful scenes than these
Plato ne'er portrayed.

3.

Subest fons vivacis vene,
Adest cantus philomene
Nayadumque cantilene.
Paradisus hic est pene;
Non sunt loca, scio plene,
His iocundiora.

4.

Hic dum placet delectari
Delectatque iocundari
Et ab estu relevari,
Cerno forma singulari
Pastorellam sine pari
Colligentem mora.

5.

In amorem vise cedo,
Fecit Venus hoc, ut credo.
"Ades," inquam, "non sum predo,
Nichil tollo, nichil ledo.
Me meaque tibi dedo
Pulchrior quam Flora."

6.

Que respondit verbo brevi:
"Ludos viri non assuevi.
Sunt parentes michi sevi;
Mater longioris evi
Irascetur pro re levi.
Parce nunc in hora!"

3.

There's a lively brooklet near,
Philomele's voice I hear,
Naiads with their song entice,
This is well-nigh paradise,
For I scarcely know a place
Sweeter in its grace.

4.

While I seek my pleasure here,
In such pleasure find good cheer
With a little rest from heat,
Soon a shepherdess I greet
Fairer than one ever sees,
Picking mulberries.

5.

Seeing her was loving her—
Venus' power, I aver—,
"Come, I am no thief, my dear,
Rob not, harm not, never fear.
What is mine I'll give you, lass,
Flora you outclass."

6.

Curtly then the maiden said:
"Games with men I've never played.
I must fear my parents' rage,
Mother is well up in age,
Lightsome ways would anger her.
Now excuse me, sir!"

2. Declinante frigore

1.

Declinante frigore
Picto terre corpore
Tellus sibi credita
Multo reddit fenore.
Eo surgens tempore
Nocte iam emerita
Resedi sub arbore.

2.

Desub ulmo patula
Manat unda garrula,
Ver ministrat gramine
Fontibus umbracula,
Qui per loca singula
Profluunt aspergine
Virgultorum pendula.

3.

Dum concentus avium
Et susurri foncium
Garriente rivulo
Per convexa moncium
Removerent tedium,
Vidi sinu patulo
Venire Glycerium.

4.

Clamis multiphario
Nitens artificio
Dependebat vertice
Cotulata vario.
Vestis erat Tyrio
Colorata murice
Opere plumario.

2. *Willing Shepherdess*   (Walther of Châtillon)

1.

When the winter's cold was gone,
When the earth with color shone,
Bringing buds and shoots to sight
As the sower's generous prize,
I decided then to rise
As the day broke up the night.
'neath a tree I sat alone.

2.

By a shady elm that rustled
Flowed a babbling brook that hustled,
Grasses high that spring days grow
Give the wellsprings shady bases
As they run through many places,
Moistening thickets as they flow,
Branches too that hang down low.

3.

While the swarms of birds that sing
Mid the fountains' whispering,
With the brooklet gurgling low
(Heard o'er mountain, dale, and lea),
Do away with all ennui,
I could see, with robes that flow
Young Glycerë nearing me.

4.

From her head a veil was pendant,
Decorative and resplendent,
Wrought with cunning artifice,
It was striped with colors bright.
In a frock she was bedight,
Made of Tyrian red was this.
Plumage set it off aright.

5.

Frons illius adzima,
Labia tenerrima.
"Ades," inquam, "omnium
Michi dilectissima,
Cor meum et anima,
Cuius forme lilium
Mea pascit intima.

6.

In te semper oscito,
Vix ardorem domito;
A me quicquid agitur,
Lego sive scriptito,
Crucior et merito,
Ni frui conceditur,
Quod constanter optito."

7.

Ad hec illa frangitur,
Humi sedit igitur,
Et sub fronde tenera,
Dum vix moram patitur,
Subici compellitur.
Sed quis nescit cetera?
Pedicatus vincitur.

3. Vere dulci mediante

1.

Vere dulci mediante,
Non in Maio, paulo ante,
Luce solis radiante,
Virgo vultu elegante
Fronde stabat sub vernante
Canens cum cicuta.

5.

While her brow was smooth and clear,
Tender did her lips appear.
"You are come," I cried with pleasure,
"Sweetest love for whom I've pined,
You my heart and you my mind,
You my lily, you my treasure,
You are ravishing, my dear.

6.

Evermore for you I languish,
Scarcely can I check my anguish;
If I work or if I toy,
Read or write—whate'er I would—,
I feel torture, as I should,
If I never can enjoy
What I seek and crave as good."

7.

Hearing this, she stops negating,
Settles on the ground while waiting,
As by foliage caressed
Willingly she bides the time,
Bound to yield beneath the lime.
Say, who doesn't know the rest?
Pederasty's not the best.

3. Shepherdess Taken by Storm

1.

While sweet spring was holding sway,
't was before the month of May,
Shining sun warmed up the day,
She, the girl with pretty face,
Midst the green leaves took her place,
Played a reed and trilled.

2.

Illuc veni fato dante.
Nympha non est forme tante,
Equipollens eius plante.
Que me viso festinante
Grege fugit cum balante,
Metu dissoluta.

3.

Clamans tendit ad ovile.
Hanc sequendo precor: "Sile,
Nichil timeas hostile!"
Preces spernit et monile,
Quod ostendi, tenet vile
Virgo sic locuta:

4.

"Munus vestrum," inquit, "nolo,
Quia pleni estis dolo."
Et se sic defendit colo.
Comprehensam ieci solo,
Clarior non est sub polo
Vilibus induta.

5.

Satis illi fuit grave,
Michi gratum et suave.
"Quid fecisti," inquit, "prave!
Ve ve tibi, tamen ave!
Ne reveles ulli, cave,
Ut sim domi tuta!

6.

Si senserit meus pater
Vel Martinus maior frater,
Erit michi dies ater,
Vel si sciret mea mater,
Cum sit angue peior quater,
Virgis sum tributa."

2.

I, fate willing, passed her there,
Nymphs with her cannot compare:
Instep, ankle, anywhere.
Seeing me and how I hurried,
With her bleating flock she scurried,
Fear her heart had filled.

3.

Wailing, for the cote she made,
Following her, "Be still," I said,
Of ill-will be not afraid!"
Pleas she spurned, and of the necklace
Which I showed her she was reckless,
Speaking in this vein:

4.

"I won't have your gift," she laughed,
"Since you act with guile and craft,"
Brandishing her shepherd's shaft.
Down I laid her to the ground,
None more fair is to be found,
Though her garb was plain.

5.

This for her was grave defeat,
Though for me 't was very sweet.
"What you've done, you wretch," in heat
Spoke she, "Woe to you, now run!
Don't breathe this to anyone,
Or at home I'll sweat.

6.

"If my father gets to hear it,
Brother Martin e'en come near it,
I'll have trouble, and I fear it,
Or if mother knew, that griper—
Four times worse than any viper—,
Floggings I would get."

4. Lucis orto sidere

1.

Lucis orto sidere
Exit virgo propere
Facie vernali,
Oves iussa regere
Baculo pastorali.

2.

Sol effundens radium
Dat calorem nimium.
Virgo speciosa
Solem vitat noxium
Sub arbore frondosa.

3.

Dum procedo paululum,
Lingue solvo vinculum:
"Salve, rege digna!
Audi, queso, servulum,
Esto michi benigna!"

4.

"Cur salutas virginem,
Que non novit hominem,
Ex quo fuit nata?
Sciat Deus, neminem
Inveni per hec prata."

5.

Forte lupus aderat,
Quem fames expulerat
Gutturis avari.
Ove rapta properat,
Cupiens saturari.

6.

Dum puella cerneret,
Quod sic ovem perderet,
Pleno clamat ore:
"Siquis ovem redderet,
Me gaudeat uxore!"

4. Shepherdess and Wolf

1.

Daytime had no sooner started
When a shepherdess departed,
Beauteous to see,
To her flock with staff she darted
Out into the lea.

2.

When the sun emits her rays
All things seem to be ablaze.
That fair maiden, she
Flees the summer's heat and haze,
Seeks a lofty tree.

3.

When the nearby spot I reach,
Shackled tongue I free for speech:
"Hail, my noble queen!
Hear your slave-man, I beseech,
Show a kindly mien!"

4.

She: "Wherefore greet this maiden, sir,
No man's yet been known to her
Since her early childhood!
God knows, ne'er did it occur
In this lonesome wildwood."

5.

Then by chance a wolf we saw,
Driven by his famished maw
Hunger pangs to stay;
Seized a lambkin with his jaw,
Hastened on his way.

6.

When it struck the shepherdess
That her lamb was in distress,
She exclaimed in anguished tone:
"Who returns my lambkin, yes,
Takes me as his own!"

7.

Mox ut vocem audio,
Denudato gladio
Lupus immolatur,
Ovis ab exicio
Redempta reportatur.

5. Exiit diluculo

1.

Exiit diluculo
    rustica puella
cum grege, cum baculo,
    cum lana novella.
Sunt in grege parvulo
    ovis et asella,
vitula cum vitulo,
    caper et capella.

2.

Conspexit in cespite
    scolarem sedere:
"quid tu facis, domine?
    veni mecum ludere!"

7.

When I heard this on the heath,
I my sword took from its sheath,
Stabbed the wolf, thus armed,
Snatched the lambkin from his teeth,
Brought it back unharmed.

5. *Shepherdess Goes Forth*

1.

Night did fade, a country maid
    From her cottage took
New-shorn wool a whole bag full
    With her flock and crook.
Midst the little flock in heather
    Ass and calf we note,
Bullock walking next to wether,
    She- and billy goat.

2.

In the grass observing her
    A student lay at ease,
"Pray, what are you doing, sir?
    Gambol with me, please!"

1. Anni parte florida

1.

Anni parte florida,
Celo puriore,
Picto terre gremio
Vario colore,
Dum fugaret sidera
Nuncius aurore,
Liquit somnus oculos
Phillidis et Flore.

2.

Placuit virginibus
Ire spaciatum,
Nam soporem reicit
Pectus sauciatum.
Equis ergo passibus
Exeunt in pratum,
Ut et locus faciat
Ludum esse gratum.

3.

Erant ambe virgines
Et ambe regine,
Phillis coma libera,
Flore compto crine.
Non sunt forme virginum,
Sed forme divine,
Et respondent facies
Luci matutine.

CHAPTER V

𝔇𝔦𝔰𝔭𝔲𝔱𝔞𝔱𝔦𝔬𝔫 𝔞𝔫𝔡 𝔓𝔞𝔯𝔬𝔡𝔶 *

1. *Phyllis and Flora*

1.

In the flowery days of spring,
When the sky was fairer,
Till the bosom of the earth
Bore hues ever rarer,
When the stars had faded out,
Yielding to Aurora,
Sleep had left the maidens two,
Phyllis fair and Flora.

2.

So the pair decided now
That a walk they'd take,
Saddened hearts rejected sleep,
Keeping them awake.
Then with measured step they found
Greening fields in fast time,
't was a pretty spot that lent
Pleasure to their pastime.

3.

Both were maidens and by birth
Princesses as well,
Phyllis' locks were flowing free,
Braided Flora's fell.
Heaven had made them beautiful,
Human beauty scorning,
Radiant their faces were,
Like the light of morning.

---

*On this chapter see the Introduction, pp. 24 ff.

4.
Nec stirpe nec facie
Nec ornatu viles
Et annos et animos
Habent iuveniles;
Sed sunt parum impares
Et parum hostiles,
Nam huic placet clericus,
Et huic placet miles.

5.
Non eis distancia
Corporis aut oris,
Omnia communia
Sunt intus et foris,
Sunt unius habitus
Et unius moris,
Sola differencia
Modus est amoris.

6.
Susurrabat modicum
Ventus tempestivus,
Locus erat viridi
Gramine festivus,
Et in ipso gramine
Defluebat rivus
Vivus atque garrulo
Murmure lascivus.

7.
Ad augmentum decoris
Et caloris minus
Fuit secus rivulum
Spaciosa pinus
Venustata folio,
Late pandens sinus,
Nec intrare poterat
Calor peregrinus.

4.

Nor in birth nor shape nor dress
Were the twain uncouth,
Both in years and spirit they
Bore the marks of youth;
But they differed just a bit,
Disagreed a mite:
Flora loved a clerical,
Phyllis loved a knight.

5.

Difference was not revealed,
Speech and build and frame:
Each was like the other one's,
Everything the same,
All their habits, attitudes
Showed the selfsame bent,
Yet in whom the maidens loved
They were different.

6.

Gentle breezes stirred a bit
Murmurous and restive,
Grasses growing everywhere
Made the place seem festive,
Through the meadow grass a brook
Flowed in exultation,
Babbling, murmuring on the way
Pertly—no cessation.

7.

Heightening their beauty still,
Routing too the heat,
Near the brooklet's course a pine
Spread its branches neat,
Bearing needles long and trim;
Screened the mead and spanned it,
Keeping out beyond approach
Onerous heat, that bandit.

8.

Consedere virgines,
Herba sedem dedit,
Phillis iuxta rivulum,
Flora longe sedit.
Et dum sedet utraque,
Dum in sese redit,
Amor corda vulnerat
Et utramque ledit.

9.

Amor est interius
Latens et occultus
Et corde certissimos
Elicit singultus;
Pallor genas inficit,
Alternantur vultus,
Sed in verecundia
Furor est sepultus.

10.

Phillis in suspirio
Floram deprehendit,
Et hanc de consimili
Flora reprehendit;
Altera sic alteri
Mutuo rependit,
Tandem morbum detegit
Et vultus ostendit.

11.

Ille sermo mutuus
Multum habet more,
Et est quedam series
Tota de amore;
Amor est in animis,
Amor est in ore.
Tandem Phillis incipit
Et arridet Flore.

8.

There the maidens took a seat,
Grasses were their mat,
Phyllis near the brook reclined,
Far off Flora sat;
While the two were squatting thus
Introspectively,
Love inflicted wounds on each
Maiden grievously.

9.

Granted, Love lies deep inside,
Hid in secret guise,
Yet he wrings from every heart
Clear unguarded sighs;
Pallor makes the cheeks turn pale,
Faces change expression,
Modesty however stirs,
Keeps concealed the passion.

10.

Phyllis catches Flora then
As a sigh she heaves,
Flora similarly hears
How her Phyllis grieves;
One detects the other thus,
Marks their mutual fate,
Each reveals her love-sick heart,
Each admits her state.

11.

But their little give and take,
Slow it is to move,
While its sequence more or less
Deals alone with love;
Only love is on their minds,
Fills their speech completely.
Phyllis then at last begins,
Smiles at Flora sweetly:

12.

"Miles," inquit, "inclite,
Mea cura Paris,
Ubi modo militas
Et ubi moraris?
O vita milicie,
Vita singularis,
Sola digna gaudio
Dionei laris!"

13.

Dum puella militem
Recolit amicum,
Flora ridens oculos
Iacit in obliquum
Et in risu loquitur
Verbum inimicum:
"Amas," inquit, "poteras
Dicere mendicum.

14.

Sed quid Alcibiades
Facit, mea cura,
Res creata dignior
Omni creatura,
Quem beavit omnibus
Graciis natura?
O sola felicia
Clericorum iura!"

15.

Floram Phillis arguit
De sermone duro
Et sermone loquitur
Floram commoturo;
Nam "Ecce virgunculam,"
Inquit, "Corde puro,
Cuius pectus nobile
Servit Epicuro!

12.

"Paris, famous knight," she says,
"Object of my yearning,
Where are you campaigning now,
Where are you sojourning?
O the military life,
Life unique and rare,
Worthy of the bliss alone
Venus can prepare!"

13.

While the maid her knightly friend
Honored thus and praised,
Flora laughed a ringing laugh,
E'en an eyebrow raised,
Then still laughing, out she spoke,
Said a hostile word:
"Beggar you could call your love,"
Tartly she averred.

14.

"How fares Alcibiades,
He, *my* love-sensation,
He, a being that outdoes
Any in creation,
He whom with all blessings rare
Nature's laws invest?
O the clericals of all
Men are happiest!"

15.

Phyllis chided Flora's speech,
Harsh and sharp of bite,
Then she uttered rousing words,
Flora to incite:
"O behold the maiden fair
With a heart so pure,
Now her noble soul must serve
Only Epicure!

16.

Surge, surge, misera,
De furore fedo!
Solum esse clericum
Epicurum credo.
Nichil elegancie
Clerico concedo,
Cuius implet latera
Moles et pinguedo.

17.

A castris Cupidinis
Cor habet remotum,
Qui somnum desiderat
Et cibum et potum.
O puella nobilis,
Omnibus est notum,
Quod est longe militis
Ab hoc voto votum.

18.

Solis necessariis
Miles est contentus,
Somno, cibo, potui
Non vivit intentus;
Amor illi prohibet,
Ne sit somnolentus,
Cibus, potus militis
Amor et iuventus.

19.

Quis amicos copulet
Nostros loro pari?
Lex, natura sineret
Illos copulari?
Meus novit ludere,
Tuus epulari,
Meo semper proprium
Dare, tuo dari."

16.

"Rise, O rise, unhappy girl,
From your madness shrink!
Clerics, only clerics are
Epicures, I think.
Elegance can never be
Any cleric's lot.
He must fill his belly up
Till it's like a pot.

17.

"From the camp of Cupid he
Keeps his heart far distant,
He on sleep and food and drink
Only is insistent.
Maiden, born of noble stock,
't is the truth long proved
That from base desires like this
Knights are e'er removed.

18.

"With necessities alone
Knights are well content,
Not on sleep or food or drink
Is their life intent;
Love would never let them be
Somnolent, in truth.
Food and drink for knightly folk
Are but love and youth.

19.

"Who would bind your friend and mine
As a pair together?
Or would Nature, which is Law,
These two ever tether?
Mine is skilled in making love,
Yours in sumptuous living,
Yours in taking generous gifts,
Mine alone in giving."

20.

Haurit Flora sanguinem
Vultu verecundo
Et apparet pulchrior
In risu secundo
Et tandem eloquio
Reserat facundo,
Quod corde conceperat
Artibus fecundo:

21.

"Satis," inquit, "libere,
Phillis, es locuta,
Multum es eloquio
Velox et acuta,
Sed non efficaciter
Verum prosecuta,
Ut per te prevaleat
Lilio cicuta.

22.

Dixisti de clerico,
Quod indulget sibi,
Servum somni nominas
Et potus et cibi.
Sic solet ab invido
Probitas describi;
Ecce, parum patere,
Respondebo tibi.

23.

Tot et tanta, fateor,
Sunt amici mei,
Quod numquam incogitat
Aliene rei.
Celle mellis, olei,
Cereris, Lyei,
Aurum, gemme, pocula
Famulantur ei.

20.

With a feeling marked by shame
Flora shyly blushed,
Then her face grew lovelier,
With a smile 't was flushed,
Till at last with eloquence
Cleverly she stated
What her richly fertile mind
Had originated:

21.

"Freely, Phyllis," then she said,
"Yes, enough you've gabbed,
With a deal of eloquence
Fast and sharp you've stabbed.
But the truth you have unveiled
Awkwardly and illy,
Since for you the hemlock rates
Higher than the lily.

22.

"Clerics you have just described—
An indulging brood—
Slaves to sleep you've said they are,
Slaves to drink and food.
Probity is thus described
By an envious crew;
Patience just a moment, please,
Then I'll answer you.

23.

"Riches has my friend so great,
This I must admit,
He desires no neighbor's wealth,
Nor has use for it.
Chambers full of honey, oil,
Grain and wine and more,
Gems and goblets too he owns,
Gold a goodly store.

24.
In tam dulci copia
Vite clericalis,
Quod non potest aliqua
Pingi voce talis,
Volat et duplicibus
Amor plaudit alis,
Amor indeficiens,
Amor immortalis.

25.
Sentit tela Veneris
Et Amoris ictus,
Non est tamen clericus
Macer aut afflictus,
Quippe nulla gaudii
Parte derelictus,
Cui respondet animus
Domine non fictus.

26.
Macer est et pallidus
Tuus preelectus,
Pauper et vix pallio
Sine pelle tectus,
Non sunt artus validi
Nec robustum pectus,
Nam cum causa deficit,
Deest et effectus.

27.
Turpis est pauperies
Imminens amanti.
Quid prestare poterit
Miles postulanti?
Sed dat multa clericus
Et ex abundanti,
Tante sunt divicie
Reditusque tanti."

24.

"To possessions rich and sweet
That the clerics hold,
That no tongue can well describe,
Since they are untold,
Love aspires and flies amain,
As his wings he tries—
Indefatigable Love,
Love that never dies.

25.

"Venus' weapons he can feel,
Love gives him a tweak,
Yet the cleric's not fatigued,
Seems not to be weak;
Joys of every kind he knows,
No recluse is he,
She that loves him, she is true
Unremittingly.

26.

"Lean is he and pale of face
Whom you call your love,
Poor, with coat that lacks of fur
Under and above,
Weak in spirit, weak of limb,
Frail in each respect:
Where a cause cannot be found
There is no effect.

27.

"Poverty's a shameful state,
To the girl a blight:
When a favor she would ask
How responds her knight?
But the cleric gives and gives,
Knows no diminution,
So abundant is his wealth,
Rich his contribution."

28.
Flore Phillis obicit:
"Multum es perita
In utrisque studiis
Et utraque vita,
Satis probabiliter
Et pulchre mentita,
Sed hec altercacio
Non quiescet ita.

29.
Cum orbem letificat
Hora lucis feste,
Tunc apparet clericus
Satis inhoneste,
In tonsura capitis
Et in atra veste
Portans testimonium
Voluptatis meste.

30.
Non est ullus adeo
Fatuus aut cecus,
Cui non appareat
Militare decus.
Tuus est in ocio
Quasi brutum pecus;
Meum terit galea,
Meum portat equus.

31.
Meus armis dissipat
Inimicas sedes,
Et si forte prelium
Solus init pedes,
Dum tenet Bucefalam
Suus Ganimedes,
Ille me commemorat
Inter ipsas cedes.

28.

Phyllis answered Flora then:
"Clever is your speech,
You know both men's aim on earth,
Life as led by each;
Thus with plausibility,
Dodges well defended
You'd dissolve this quarrel now,
But 't is far from ended.

29.

"When the hour of festive spring
Bids the earth be glad,
Then the cleric shows himself
Quite untimely clad,
On his head the tonsure's seen,
Black are all his clothes,
Proving thus that gladsome joy's
Happiness he loathes.

30.

"No one is so much a fool,
No one is so blind
That in military life
Glamor he'll not find.
Your beloved, in idleness,
Seems like brutish cattle,
Mine, with helmet on his head,
Rides a horse to battle.

31.

"Mine with weapons dissipates
Foes that he may meet;
If then singly into strife
He should set his feet,
While his horse Bucephalus
By his squire is led,
He still gives a thought to me
In the duel dread.

32.

Redit fusis hostibus
Et pugna confecta
Et me sepe respicit
Galea reiecta.
Ex his et ex aliis
Racione recta
Est vita milicie
Michi preelecta."

33.

Novit iram Phillidis
Et pectus anhelum
Et remittit multiplex
Illi Flora telum.
"Frustra," dixit, "loqueris
Os ponens in celum
Et per acum niteris
Figere camelum.

34.

Mel pro felle deseris
Et pro falso verum,
Que probas miliciam
Reprobando clerum.
Facit amor militem
Strenuum et ferum?
Non, immo pauperies
Et defectus rerum.

35.

Pulchra Phillis, utinam
Sapienter ames
Nec veris sentenciis
Amplius reclames!
Tuum domat militem
Et sitis et fames,
Quibus mortis petitur
Et inferni trames.

32.

"Back he comes, the foe in rout,
When the fight is over,
Then, his helmet doffed, he oft
Smiles at me, his lover.
Due to this and other things,
If I have not erred,
Knights and their careers by me
Are to be preferred."

33.

Flora noticed Phyllis' wrath,
Saw her bosom churning,
Shot the many weapons back,
Them to her returning.
" 't is in vain your voice," she said,
"Rises to the sky,
You would force the camel, dear,
Through the needle's eye.

34.

"Honey you'd replace with gall,
Truth with lies you hide
If you would applaud the knights
But the clerics chide.
Is it love that makes the knight
Strong and bold and vaunted?
No! It's poverty—he lacks
Things he's always wanted.

35.

"Lovely Phyllis, O I wish
You'd love more discreetly,
Cease objecting to remarks
That are uttered meetly!
Thirst and hunger hold your knight
Ever in their spell,
These are found upon the road
Marked for death and hell.

36.

Multum est calamitas
Militis attrita,
Sors illius dura est
Et in arto sita,
Cuius est in pendulo
Dubioque vita,
Ut habere valeat
Vite requisita.

37.

Non dicas opprobrium,
Si cognoscas morem,
Vestem nigram clerici,
Comam breviorem;
Habet ista clericus
Ad summum honorem,
Ut sese significet
Omnibus maiorem.

38.

Universa clerico
Constat esse prona,
Et signum imperii
Portat in corona.
Imperat militibus
Et largitur dona:
Famulante maior est
Imperans persona.

39.

Ociosum clericum
Semper esse iuras:
Viles spernit operas,
Fateor, et duras;
Sed cum eius animus
Evolat ad curas,
Celi vias dividit
Et rerum naturas.

36.

"Face to face with many a trial
Knights are ever brought,
Thus their lot is inhumane,
Oft with danger fraught;
Constantly uncertainty
Dogs their very life
In acquiring what they need
For their life of strife.

37.

"If you better were informed,
This you would not scorn:
That the cleric's clothes are black,
That his head is shorn;
With this most distinguished garb
Every cleric's blessed.
Thus he shows that clerics are
Better than the rest.

38.

"Clerics everyone respects,
Honor to them shows,
All insignia of power
In their crown repose.
Knights obey the cleric's word,
Gifts they take from him:
Servants all perform their lord's
Every wish and whim.

39.

"That the clerics like their ease,
This you also claim:
True, they spurn the hardest chores,
Tasks to cause them shame;
Yet when on more serious things
They would have reliance,
They can trace the paths of stars,
Probe the ways of science.

40.

Meus est in purpura,
Tuus in lorica,
Tuus est in prelio,
Meus in lectica,
Ubi gesta principum
Relegit antiqua,
Scribit, querit, cogitat
Totum de amica.

41.

Quid Dione valeat
Et amoris deus,
Primus novit clericus
Et instruxit meus;
Factus est per clericum
Miles Cithereus.
His est et huiusmodi
Tuus sermo reus."

42.

Liquit Flora pariter
Vocem et certamen
Et sibi Cupidinis
Exigit examen.
Phillis primum obstrepit,
Acquiescit tamen,
Et probato iudice
Redeunt per gramen.

43.

Totum in Cupidine
Certamen est situm;
Suum dicunt iudicem
Verum et peritum,
Quia vite noverit
Utriusque ritum;
Et iam sese preparant,
Ut eant auditum.

40.

"Mine is clad in purple garb,
Yours in mail instead,
Yours is on the battle ground,
Mine remains in bed,
Where he reads of exploits old
Wrought by many an earl,
Where he writes and asks and thinks
Only of his girl.

41.

"What Dionë can achieve,
Cupid too can do,
That my cleric taught the world,
That he only knew.
Cleric 't was who gave the knight
Cytherean bent.
Unbeknown your words have proved
This, their real intent."

42.

Flora now abstained from both:
Speech and disputation,
Asked that Cupid give the case
Fair examination;
Phyllis raised objection first,
Later acquiesced,
Then agreeing on the judge,
Home through grass they pressed.

43.

Fully into Cupid's hands
Was the matter placed,
Him they thought with truthfulness,
Much experience graced,
Since the two men's mode of life
Well he knew—their way;
Straightway they set out to hear
What he'd have to say.

. . . . *

72.

Inter hec aspicitur
Cytheree natus;
Vultus est sidereus,
Vertex est pennatus,
Arcum leva possidet
Et sagittas latus,
Satis potest conici
Potens et elatus.

73.

Sceptro puer nititur
Floribus perplexo,
Stillat odor nectaris
De capille pexo;
Tres assistunt Gracie
Digito connexo,
Et amoris calicem
Tenent genu flexo.

74.

Appropinquant virgines
Et adorant tute
Deum venerabili
Cinctum iuventute,
Gloriantur numinis
In tanta virtute.
Quas deus considerans
Prevenit salute.

*See English text on facing page; strophes 44–71 add nothing to
the plot and are omitted.

[*The girls depart on their mission, Phyllis on a most unusual mule, a gift to her mother from Venus, who had
in turn received it from Neptune; Flora on an elegantly
caparisoned horse which had been broken in with the
reins of Pegasus and decked out by Vulcan and Minerva.
Thus mounted, the maidens travel to Cupid's paradise,
where sensuous attractions greet them—music of instru-
ments and birds, and choirs of devotees of love. The
maidens too are amorously affected. Finally they encoun-
ter god Cupid himself surrounded by fauns, nymphs,
and satyrs.*]

72.

There is Cytherea's son
In their midst discovered,
Starry was his countenance,
Plumes his proud head covered,
In his left were arrows sharp,
At his side a bow;
That he was a mighty god
Everyone could know.

73.

On his scepter there he leans,
Decked with flowers rare,
While the scent of nectar wafts
From his wavy hair;
There with hands that intertwine
Stand the graces three,
Offering the cup of love,
Each on bended knee.

74.

Closer came the maidens now,
Both in proper mood,
Venerate the mighty god
Young, with charm endued.
So all-powerful was he
That this god must awe them.
He, expecting their approach,
Nodded when he saw them.

75.
Causam vie postulat;
Aperitur causa,
Et laudatur utraque
Tantum pondus ausa.
Ad utramque loquitur:
"Modo parum pausa,
Donec res iudicio
Reseretur clausa!"

76.
Deus erat; virgines
Norunt deum esse,
Retractari singula
Non fuit necesse.
Equos suos deserunt
Et quiescunt fesse.
Amor suis imperat,
Iudicent expresse.

77.
Amor habet iudices,
Amor habet iura,
Sunt Amoris iudices
Usus et Natura;
Istis tota data est
Curie censura,
Quoniam preterita
Sciunt et futura.

78.
Eunt et iusticie
Ventilant vigorem,
Ventilatum retrahunt
Curie rigorem;
Secundum scienciam
Et secundum morem
Ad amorem clericum
Dicunt apciorem.

75.

Cupid asks them why they've come,
They their reason state,
He extols their bringing forth
Matters of such weight.
Then to both he speaks these words:
"Not long will you bide
Till a verdict springs the lock,
This case to decide!"

76.

Cupid was a god, no doubt,
Both the maidens knew it:
Needless to rehearse the case,
Once more go all through it.
They dismounted from their steeds
Wearily, then rested.
Cupid ordered now the case
Judged as they requested.

77.

Cupid has of judges twain,
Laws for judicature,
These two judges wise are called
Usage, yea, and Nature;
They alone are arbiters,
From them judgments flow,
They can look into the past,
They the future know.

78.

They proceed and all the law's
Vigor they pursue,
Air the court's fixed rules of thumb,
Precedents review;
In accord with what is known,
Practices well rooted,
They declare: to clerics is
Love much better suited.

79.
Comprobavit curia
Diccionem iuris
Et teneri voluit
Eciam futuris.
Parum ergo precavent
Rebus nocituris,
Que sequuntur militem
Et fatentur pluris.

2. In illo tempore:

Inicium sancti evangelii secundum marcas argenti.

Il illo tempore (Hic incipiunt Evangelii pericope) dixit papa Romanis:
"*Cum venerit filius hominis* (Mt. 25, 31) ad sedem *maiestatis* nostre, primum dicite: '*Amice, ad quid venisti*' (Mt. 26, 50)?

At ille si perseveraverit pulsans (Lc. 11, 4), nil dans vobis, *eicite* eum in tenebras *exteriores* (Mt. 25, 30)!"

Factum est autem (Lc. 1, 8, etc.), ut quidam pauper clericus veniret ad curiam domini pape, et *exclamavit dicens* (Mt. 15, 22, etc.):
"*Miseremini mei saltem vos,* hostiarii pape, *quia manus paupertatis tetigit me* (Job 19, 21). *Ego vero egenus et pauper sum* (Ps. 69, 6), ideo peto, ut subveniatis *calamitati et miserie* (Zeph. 1, 15) mee."

Illi autem *audientes indignati sunt* (Mt. 20, 24) valde et dixerunt:
"*Amice, paupertas tua tecum sit in perdicione* (Act. 8, 20). *Vade retro satanas, quia non sapis* (Mc. 8, 33), ea, *que* sapiunt nummi.

79.

Courtiers lauded this decree
By the judges spoken,
Wished that it in future should
Stand and ne'er be broken.—
Men run risk of injury,
As they soon discover,
Thinking: knights perhaps outdo
Clerics playing lover.

2. At That Time:

Beginning of the Holy Gospel of the Mark of Silver

At that time (beginning of the Gospel pericopes) the
Pope spoke to his Romans:
"*When the son of man shall come to our seat of glory*
(Matt. 25, 31), then say first: *'Friend, wherefore art
thou come?'* (Matt. 26, 50).

But if he continues knocking, giving you nothing, *cast
ye* him *into outer darkness* (Matt. 25, 30)!"

And it came to pass (Luke 1, 8) that a certain poor cleric
came to the curia of the lord Pope and *cried unto him,
saying* (Matt. 15, 22):
"*Have pity upon me*, ye gate-keepers of the Pope, *for
the hand of poverty has touched me* (Job 19, 21). *But
I am poor and sorrowful* (Ps. 69, 29), therefore I beg
you to help me in my *wasteness and desolation* (Zeph.
1, 15)."

When they *heard it, they were moved with indignation*
(Matt. 20, 24) and said:
"Friend, thy poverty *perish with thee* (Acts 8, 20). *Get
thee behind me Satan: for thou savorest not the things
that* (Mark 8, 33) money savors.

Amen, *amen, dico tibi:* non intrabis in gaudium domini tui, *donec* dederis *novissimum quadrantem* (Mt. 5, 26)."

Pauper vero *abiit et vendidit* (Mt. 13, 46) *pallium et tunicam* (1. Esra 9, 4) et *universa, que habuit* (Mt. 13, 44), et dedit cardinalibus et hostiariis et camerariis.

At illi dixerunt: "Et hoc *quid est inter tantos* (Job 6, 9)?"

Et *eiecerunt eum ante fores* (Jo. 9, 34), *et egressus foras flevit amare* (Mt. 26, 75) et *non habens consolacionem* (Thren. 1, 9).

Posta venit ad curiam *quidam* clericus dives, *incrassatus, impinguatus, dilatatus* (Deut. 32, 15), *qui* propter *sedicionem fecerat homicidium* (Mc. 15, 7).

Hic primo dedit hostiario, secundo, camerario tercio cardinalibus. At illi *arbitrati sunt* inter eos, *quod essent plus accepturi* (Mt. 20, 10).

Audiens autem dominus papa cardinales et ministros *plurima dona* (Prov. 6, 35) a clerico accepisse, *infirmatus est usque ad mortem* (Phil. 2, 27).

Dives vero misit sibi electuarium aureum et argenteum, *et statim sanatus est* (Jo. 5, 9).

Tunc dominus papa *ad se vocavit* (Mt. 20, 25) cardinales et ministros et dixit eis:

"Fratres, videte, ne (Hebr. 3, 12) aliquis *vos seducat inanibus verbis* (Eph. 5, 6).

Exemplum enim do vobis, ut, quemadmodum ego capio, *ita et vos* capiatis (Jo. 13, 15)."

Verily, verily I say unto thee, thou shalt by no means come to the joy of thy lord, *till thou hast paid the uttermost farthing* (Matt. 5, 26)."

The poor man *went out and sold* (Matt. 13, 46) coat And tunic and *all that he hath* (Matt. 13, 44) and gave it to the cardinals and gate-keepers and chamberlains.

And they said: "*What is that among so many* (Job 6, 9)?"

And they cast him out (John 9, 34) before the door *and he went out and wept bitterly* (Matt. 26, 75) and *had no comforter* (Lam. 1, 9).

Then there came to the curia a certain rich cleric, *waxen fat, grown thick, covered with fatness* (Deut. 32, 15) *who had committed murder in the insurrection* (Mark 15, 7).

He gave first to the gate-keeper, then to the chamberlain, thirdly to the cardinals. But *they supposed they should have received more* (Matt. 20, 10).

The lord Pope, hearing that the cardinals and servants had received *many gifts* (Prov. 6, 35) from the cleric, *was sick nigh unto death* (Phil. 2, 27).

But the rich man sent him medicine of gold and silver and *immediately the man was made whole* (John 5, 9).

Then the lord Pope *called unto him* (Matt. 20, 25) the cardinals and servants and said to them:

"*Take heed brethren* (Heb. 3, 12), *let no man deceive you with vain words* (Eph. 5, 6).

For I have given you an example, that ye shall do as I have done to you (John 13, 15)."

CHAPTER VI

History, Folklore, and Amour

POEMS 1–5 in this chapter, like 1 and 2 in Chapter III, are found in the Cambridge Songs (Nos. 11, 14, 15, 20 and 48). These five all seem to be German in origin. Poems 1–3 are written in the form of the sequence of the Roman Catholic service. In a sequence, pairs of successive strophes correspond to each other in structure. For example, in poem 1, strophes 1a and 1b have ten lines each, 2a and 2b have eight, and 7 is an orphan. The subjects of these poems (2–4) were old favorites in the monastic schools.

The term "modus" in the titles of the first three means melody and text of historical or anecdotal poems. We find *modi* mentioned around 1030 by Master Ebo of Worms to King Henry III of Germany, who was interested in them and cultivated them at his court. It seems possible then that the *modi* in the Cambridge Songs (seven in all) are traceable to Henry's court. "Modus Ottinc" awkwardly glorifies Emperor Otto I (912–973), but more specifically Otto III, and could have been written for the latter's imperial coronation on May 21, 996. This may be one of the oldest poems in the present collection; in view of the early date, the author's Teutonic pride is surprising. "Modus Liebinc" deals with a familiar absurd legend in a pleasant manner, while "Modus Florum" is a typical prankster's or prevaricator's tale, called in German *Schwabenstreich,* or Swabian prank. "The She-Ass of Alfrad," written in rhythmic adonics, might be taken for an allegory, were it not so naively pointless. Its localization gives it an air of authenticity. "To a Boy" is a traditional *paidikon,* addressed to the poet's favorite young lad and suggesting pederasty; the author hails from the north Italian region of the Adige (Etsch) river, then still essentially Germanic. Its meter is the alexandrine, at the time (in the eleventh

1. Magnus cesar Otto (Modus Ottinc)

1a.

Magnus cesar Otto,
quem hic modus refert
in nomine,
Ottinc dictus,
quadam nocte
somno membra
dum collocat,
palatium
casu subito
inflammatur.

1b.

Stant ministri, tremunt,
timent dormientem
attingere
et cordarum
pulsu facto
excitatum
salvificant
et domini
nomen carmini
inponebant.

century) still rare, and a single rhyme carries through each strophe. The Greek expressions and the generally learned and bombastic style stamp it as a typically monkish tour de force.

The last two poems in this chapter, by Hugh of Orléans (see Chapter I, poems 3–5), are discussed in the Introduction (p. 28). They are satirical in content and intent and throw light upon social conditions during the early twelfth century.

1. Otto Mode

1a.
The great Caesar Otto,
whom this mode [song]
deals with,
called "Ottinc" by name—
on a certain night
while he rests his limbs
in sleep,
his palace
by a sudden chance
is enveloped in flames.

1b.
His servants stand, they tremble,
they fear to touch
the sleeper,
and they rescue him
by arousing him
with plucking
of strings
and then gave their master's
name to the song
they play.

2a.

Excitatus
spes suis surrexit,
timor magnus
adversis mox venturus;
nam tunc fama volitat
Ungarios
signa in eum
extulisse.

2b.

Iuxta litus
sedebant armati,
urbes, agros,
villas vastant late,
matres plorant filios
et filii
matres undique
exulari.

3a.

"Segnis ego," dixerat
Otto, "videor Parthis,
diu diu milites
tardos moneo frustra.
Dum ego demoror,
crescit clades semper.
Ergo moras rumpite
et Parthicis
mecum hostibus
obviate!"

2a.

Aroused,
he arose—he a hope for them,
soon to approach
as a great fear
to his foes;
for at that time the rumor flies
that the Hungarians [Huns]
had raised their standards against him.

2b.

Near the shore
they lodged their arms,
they devastate cities,
fields, villages far and wide,
mothers lament that their sons,
and sons
that their mothers
were driven into exile.

3a.

"Indolent I seem to the Parthians [Huns],"
said Otto,
"for a long, long time
I admonish my delinquent soldiers in vain,
as long as I delay
the carnage will ever increase.
Therefore break the delay
and with me
rush to meet
the Parthian foes!"

3b.
Dux Cuonrat intrepidus,
quo non fortior alter:
"Miles," inquit, "pereat,
quem hoc terreat bellum.
Arma induite,
armis instant hostes,
ipse ergo signifer
effudero
primus sanguinem
inimicum."

4a.
His incensi
bella fremunt,
arma poscunt,
hostes vocant,
signa secuntur,
tubis canunt,
clamor passim oritur
et milibus
centum Teutones
inmiscentur.

4b.
Pauci cedunt,
plures cadunt,
Francus instat,
Parthus fugit,
vulgus exangue
undis obstat;
Licus rubens sanguine
Danubio
cladem Parthicam
ostendebat.

3b.

Duke Conrad, the fearless,
than whom no one was braver,
"Let that soldier," he says, "perish
whom this war terrifies.
Take up your arms,
the enemy take to theirs,
then I as standard bearer
will myself
as the first one
spill the enemy's blood."

4a.

Stirred by these words,
they shout war,
demand arms,
call the enemy,
follow the standards,
sing to the horns;
everywhere tumult arises,
and among a thousand foes
a hundred Teutons
mingle.

4b.

Few yield,
many fall,
the Frank presses on,
the Hun flees,
the bloodless [dead] heap
stops the waves;
the river Lech, red with blood,
revealed
to the Danube
the slaughter of the Parthians.

5a.
Parva manu
cesis Parthis
ante et post
sepe victor
communem cunctis
movens luctum
nomen, regnum, optimos
hereditans
mores filio
obdormivit.

5b.
Adolescens
post hunc Otto
imperavit
multis annis
cesar iustus
clemens fortis,
unum modo defuit;
nam inclitis
raro preliis
triumphabat.

6a.
Eius autem
clara proles
Otto, decus
iuventutis,
ut fortis, ita
felix erat;
arma quos numquam militum
domuerant,
fama nominis
satis vicit.

5a.

[As] the Parthians were slaughtered
by a small force,
[so] he was often a victor
before and after;
causing common
grief to all,
he left
his name, his kingdom, his nobles,
and ways to his own son
and died.

5b.

After him
the youth Otto
ruled
for many years,
a just Caesar,
kind, brave,
but lacking only in one respect:
for he rarely
triumphed
in famous battles.

6a.

But this famous
offspring
Otto, an adornment
of youth,
as brave as
he was fortunate—
those whom the arms of soldiery never
conquered
were conquered fully
by the fame of his name.

6b.
Bello fortis,
pace potens,
in utroque
tamen mitis,
inter triumphos,
bella, pacem
semper suos pauperes
respexerat,
inde pauperum
pater fertur.

7.
Finem modo demus,
ne forte notemur
ingenii culpa
tantorum virtutes
ultra quicquam
deterere,
quas denique
Maro inclitus
vix equaret.

2. Advertite, omnes populi   (Modus Liebinc)

1a.
Advertite,
omnes populi,
ridiculum
et audite, quomodo
Suevum mulier
et ipse illam
defraudaret.

6b.

Brave in war,
powerful in peace,
in both
however gentle;
among triumphs,
wars, peace
he always took consideration
of his poor,
wherefore he was called
father of the poor.

7.

Let us now reach the end,
lest perchance we be censured
that for lack of intelligence
we detracted
beyond measure
from the nobility of such men—
nobility to which even
famous Maro [Vergil]
could scarcely do justice.

2. *The Snow Child*

1a.

Hear,
all ye people,
the laughable event,
and listen how
a wife deceived
a Swabian,
and he her.

1b.

Constantie
civis Suevulus
trans equora
gazam portans navibus
domi coniugem
lascivam nimis
relinquebat.

2a.

Vix remige
triste secat mare,
ecce subito
orta tempestate
furit pelagus,
certant flamina,
tolluntur fluctus,
post multaque exulem
vagum littore
longinquo nothus
exponebat.

2b.

Nec interim
domi vacat coniux;
mimi aderant,
iuvenes secuntur,
quos et inmemor
viri exulis
excepit gaudens
atque nocte proxima
pregnans filium
iniustum fudit
iusto die.

1b.

From Constance
a Swabian citizen,
transporting goods in ships
across the sea,
left
his too lascivious
wife at home.

2a.

With difficulty his vessel
cuts the desolate sea
with its oarsmen,
when suddenly
a tempest arises
and the ocean rages,
the winds vie with each other
and the waves mount,
and after a long while
the south wind casts the straying exile
on a distant shore.

2b.

But meanwhile
the wife was not idle at home;
mimes attended her,
young men follow her,
whom she, forgetful
of her absent husband,
gladly received;
and pregnant,
the next night
bore an unrightful son
on the rightful day.

3a.

Duobus
volutis annis
exul dictus
revertitur.
Occurrit
infida coniux
secum trahens
puerulum.
Datis osculis
maritus illi:
"De quo," inquit, "puerum
istum habeas,
dic, aut extrema
patieris."

3b.

At illa
maritum timens
dolos versat
in omnia.
"Mi," tandem,
"mi coniux," inquit,
"una vice
in Alpibus
nive sitiens
extinxi sitim.
Inde ergo gravida
istum puerum
damnoso foetu
heu gignebam."

3a.

After two
years were up,
the said absent husband
returns,
the unfaithful wife
meets him,
taking the little lad
with her.
After kisses were given,
the husband says to her:
"From whom do you have
this boy,
tell me, or you will suffer
the worst."

3b.

But she,
fearing her husband,
applies deceit
to everything.
"My husband, my husband,"
she says at last,
"once
in the Alps
I was thirsty
and quenched my thirst with snow.
Pregnant as a result of that,
then I bore
this boy,
alas, in a damnable childbirth."

4a.
Anni post hec quinque
transierunt aut plus
et mercator vagus
instauravit remos,
ratim quassam reficit,
vela alligat
et nivis natum
duxit secum.

4b.
Transfretato mari
producebat natum
et pro arrabone
mercatori tradens
centum libras accipit
atque vendito
infante dives
revertitur.

5a.
Ingressusque domum
ad uxorem ait:
"Consolare, coniux,
consolare, cara;
natum tuum perdidi,
quem non ipsa tu
me magis quidem
delexisti.

5b.
Tempestate orta
nos ventosus furor
in vadosa sirtes
nimis fessos egit,
et nos omnes graviter
torret sol, at il-
le nivis natus
liquescebat."

4a.
After this five years
or more passed
and the seafaring merchant
readied his oars again,
repairs his shattered craft,
fastens the sails,
and took the snowborn
lad along.

4b.
After the sea had been crossed,
he brought forth the boy
and, handing him over to a merchant
for a price,
accepted one hundred pounds,
then, having sold
the child, returns
rich.

5a.
And entering the house,
he said to his wife:
"Console yourself,
my dear,
I have lost your child,
whom you yourself
loved no more
than I did.

5b.
When a storm arose,
a furious gale drove us,
all tired out,
to shallow Syrtes [sandbanks],
and the sun parched
us all terribly,
but the child born of snow
melted away."

6.

Sic perfidam
Suevus coniugem
deluserat,
sic fraus fraudem vicerat;
nam quem genuit
nix, recte hunc sol
liquefecit.

3. Mendosam quam cantilenam   (Modus Florum)

1.

Mendosam quam cantilenam ago,
puerulis commendatam dabo,
quo modulos per mendaces risum
auditoribus ingentem ferant.

2a.

Liberalis et decora
cuidam regi erat nata,
quam sub lege huius modi
procis obponit querendam:

2b.

Si quis mentiendi gnarus
usque ad eo instet fallendo,
dum cesaris ore fallax
predicitur, is ducat filiam.

3a.

Quo audito Suevus
nil moratus infit:
"Raptis armis ego
dum venatum solus irem,
lepusculus inter feras
telo tactus occumbebat.
Mox effusis intestinis
caput avulsum cum cute cedo.

6.

Thus the Swabian
deceived
his faithless wife,
thus fraud conquered fraud;
because whom snow had born,
rightly did the sun
melt him.

3. *The Lying Hero*

1.

The song of fible [fable] that I take up
I shall offer as a commendation to young people,
so that, through lying verses,
they may induce mighty laughter in listeners.

2a.

A noble and decorous daughter
was born to a certain king,
whom he offered to suitors to be wooed
under the following condition:

2b.

If any man versed in lying
should in his deception go so far
as to be called a liar by the ruler,
that one shall take his daughter.

3a.

When he heard this, a Swabian
began without delay:
"As I took up my arms
and went alone to go hunting,
a little hare in the thicket
was hit by my weapon and fell.
Soon I ripped out its intestines
and, skinning the head, cut it off.

3b.

Cumque cesum manu
levaretur caput,
lesa aure effunduntur
mellis modii centeni
sotiaque auris tacta
totidem pisarum fudit.
Quibus intra pellem strictis
lepus ipse dum secatur,
crepidine summa caude
kartam regiam latentem cepi,

4.

Que servum te firmat esse meum!"—
"Mentitur," clamat rex, "karta et tu!"—

Sic rege deluso Suevus falsa
gener regius est arte factus.

4. Est unus locus

1.

Est unus locus   Homburh dictus,
in quo pascebat   asinam Alfrad,
viribus fortem   atque fidelem.

2.

Que dum in amplum   exiret campum,
vidit currentem   lupum voracem,
caput abscondit,   caudam ostendit.

3.

Lupus accurrit,   caudam momordit
asina bina   levavit crura
fecitque longum   cum lupo bellum.

4.

Cum defecisse   vires sensisset,
protulit grandem   plangendo vocem
vocansque suam   moritur domnam.

3b.

And when the head, cut off
by my hand, was lifted,
there poured from the injured ear
one hundred measures of honey,
and the companion [other] ear, when touched,
spilled forth as many peas.
After these were bound together in the skin
and the hare itself was cut up,
from the very tip of the tail
I took a hidden royal note,

4.

which asserts that you (O king) are my servant!"
"It lies," cries the king, "the card as well as you!"

Thus the Swabian deluded the king
and by a false ruse became the royal son-in-law.

4. *The She-Ass of Alfrad*

1.

There is a place, Homburg 't is called,
Where the she-ass of Alfrad, the maiden, is stalled,
Great in strength and ever loyal.

2.

While frisking about in the meadow spacious,
A wolf came running rapacious, voracious;
She hid her head but showed her tail.

3.

The wolf approached, the tail he pricked,
Her hind legs poised, the she-ass kicked
And with the wolf fought a battle long.

4.

But when she felt that her strength was spent,
With lugubrious braying the air she rent.
Calling for help to her mistress, she perished.

5.

Audiens grandem   asine vocem
Alfrad cucurrit: "Sorores," dixit,
"cito venite,   me adiuvate!

6.

Asinam caram   misi ad erbam;
illius magnum   audio planctum;
spero, cum sevo   ut pugnet lupo."

7.

Clamor sororum   venit in claustrum,
turbe virorum   ac mulierum
assunt, cruentum   ut captent lupum.

8.

Adela namque,   soror Alfrade,
Rikilam querit,   Agatham invenit,
ibant, ut fortem   sternerent hostem.

9.

At ille ruptis   asine costis
sanguinis undam   carnemque totam
simul voravit,   silvam intravit.

10.

Illud videntes   cuncte sorores
crines scindebant,   pectus tundebant,
flentes insontem   asine mortem.

11.

Denique parvum   portabat pullum;
illum plorabat   maxime Alfrad
sperans exinde   prolem crevisse.

12.

Adela mitis,   Fritherun dulcis
venerunt ambe,   ut Alverade
cor confirmarent   atque sanarent:

13.

"Delinque mestas,   soror, querelas!
Lupus amarum   non curat fletum;
Dominus aliam   dabit tibi asinam."

5.

Hearing the beast's laments as it died,
Alfrad dashed hither: "Sisters," she cried,
"Hurry, O come, I need your help!

6.

I sent my dear ass to pasture and graze,
Just now a cry I heard her raise,
I fear she is battling the terrible wolf."

7.

The sisters' shrieks pierced the cloister walls,
Both men and women heard the calls
And came to catch the cruel wolf.

8.

Adela, sister of Alfrada,
Sought Rikila and found Agatha;
They went to fell the hardy foe.

9.

The ass's ribs were broken in two,
Her flesh consumed, her bloodstream too,
The wolf then strolled into the woods.

10.

When this they saw, Alfrad and the rest,
They tore their hair and beat their breast,
Mourning the innocent ass's death.

11.

The ass had expected a little foal,
This saddened Alfrad in heart and soul,
She'd hoped a tiny ass to have.

12.

Adela, the mild, Fritherun, the dear,
Both came their Alverad to cheer,
To raise her spirit and gladden her:

13.

"Your sad lamenting, sister, quit,
The wolf will not be moved by it.
Another she-ass the lord will give."

5. O admirabile Veneris idolum

1.

O admirabile Veneris idolum,
cuius materie nihil est frivolum,
archos te protegat, qui stellas et polum
fecit et maria condidit et solum.
Furis ingenio non sentias dolum,
Cloto te diligat, que baiolat colum.

2.

"Salvato puerum" non per ipotesim,
sed firmo pectore deprecor Lachesim,
sororem Atropos, ne curet heresim.
Neptunum comitem habeas et Tetim,
cum vectus fueris per fluvium Tesim.
Quo fugis, amabo, cum te dilexerim.
Miser quid faciam, cum te non viderim?

3.

Dura materies ex matris ossibus
creavit homines iactis lapidibus,
ex quibus unus est iste puerulus,
qui lacrimabiles non curat gemitus.
Cum tristis fuero, gaudebit emulus.
Ut cerva rugio, cum fugit hinnulus.

5. *To a Boy*

1.

O admirable shape of Lady Venus' grace,
In whom no flaw I find, no blemish I can trace,
May Archos shield you who the stars and firmament
And earth and sea designed in all their vast extent.
May no such guile cloud you as prompts a thief to steal,
May Clotho love you, she who bears the spinning wheel.

2.

"Protect the lad!"—t' is not a vain hypothesis!—
I pray for you with all my heart to Lachesis;
Her sister Atropos, may ever she direct you,
May Neptune lend his hand and, guiding you, protect
you;
When on the Adije, may Thetis watch above you.
I've always cherished you, where you may go, I love you.
I, wretch, what shall I do when I no more behold you?

3.

Hard matter 't was that shaped from that Great Mother's
bones
The human race that owes its life to rocks and stones.
Among those people we may find our little lad
Who weeps no tears, who knows no lamentation sad.
My rival gloats o'er me when I with grief am shaken;
My moan is like the hind's when by the stag forsaken.

6. Quid luges, lirice

Quid luges, lirice, quid meres pro meretrice?
Respira, retice neque te dolor urat, amice!
Scimus—et est aliquid—, quia te tua Flora reliquit.
Sed tu ne cures, possunt tibi dicere plures,
Qui simili more, simili periere dolore.
Teque dolor scorti dabit afflictum cito morti,
Ne dure sorti respondes pectore forti.
Quod mala sors prebet, sapiens contempnere debet;
Res quociens mestas non est mutare potestas,
Mesta ferendo bene reddit paciencia lene.
Sed quin perferimus, quod permutare nequimus!
Consolare lyra luctum, quem parturit ira!
Paulum respira, quia destino dicere mira!
Ergo quiesce parum! Nec erit grave sic nec amarum,
Si nunc ignarum mores doceamus earum.

Lenonem lena non diligit absque crumena.
Lance cibo plena vinum fundente lagena
Plus gaudet cena quam dulce sonante Camena.
Cum nidor naso veniet, gaudebit omaso
Aut aliqua sorde plus quam dulcedine corde.

6. *Consolation for the Poet*   (Hugh of Orléans)

"Poet, why the lament? Could losing a wench so concern
                              you?
Hush, breathe easy, my friend, and let your distress
                              never burn you!
't is momentous, we know, that Flora, your sweetest,
                              you've lost,
Yet let it grieve you no whit," so speak many friends
                              you'll accost,
People who've lived like you, who of similar sorrow have
                              "perished."
Quickly will "death" overtake you when losing the
                              wench that you cherished,
If with a heart that is bold you resist not your pitiless
                              fortune.
Wise men scorn harsh fate, they neither lament nor
                              importune;
Lacking the power to change an evil that man cannot
                              alter,
We are blessed by patience to bear it and never to falter.
Let us endure what cannot be changed, let's bear it
                              serenely!
Only the lyre assuages the grief that smarts ever keenly.
Hold your breath while I speak, I'll be your tale-bearing
                              bard!
Quiet a little, I beg, 't is a task neither bitter nor hard
When we instruct newcomers in ways pursued by the
                              wenches.

Wenches will rarely make up to a lover whose credit is
                              scanter,
Boards must be loaded with food and wine from a
                              brimming decanter:
Dinner they love far more than music, whatever the type.
When the aroma approaches their nose, they will relish
                              the tripe
Or a plateful of rubbish, but music, it has no appeal.

Cum vestis danda vel erit bona cena paranda,
Tunc quidvis manda, tunc semper erit tibi blanda.
Sed cum dona feret, que nunc tibi blanda coheret,
Quem voret et laceret pociorem perfida queret.
Quo semel invento te munere linquet adempto,
Cedet contempto te paupere teque redempto.
Que predam nacta, cum res fuerit tua fracta,
Nec bona transacta tua nec recolet bene facta.
Tu risus plebis mecho ridente dolebis,
Risus eris ville, meretrix ridebit et ille.
Nescit enim miseris misereri mens mulieris
Mobilibus pueris ventoque simillima veris.
Quam quia nil dederis, modici sonus auferet eris,
Promittas rursus, velox erit inde recursus.
Si tibi bursa sonet, que spem modicam sibi donet,
Bursa redire monet, revolabit eumque reponet.
Nec nisi mendicum mendax dimittit amicum.
Bursa vocat mecham, veluti vocat ad cirotecam
Crus avis excisum vel visa caruncula nisum.
Sumpto quadrante tunc iurabit tibi sancte:
"Non dimittam te, nisi me dimiseris ante."

Give them a dress to wear or cook them a savory meal,
Soon they will be at your call for whatever favor you beg.
But while taking your gift and playing your sweet-
tempered Meg,
Faithless they'll scent out a wealthier lover to gouge and
deceive.
Then, having found him, they'll take your presents and
with him will leave.
Thus will she spurn you, the pauper, and sell you,
betraying your trust,
Finding a better prey when your assets have turned into
dust;
All the favors you showered, the kindly deeds she'll
forget,
While you, scorned by the people, despised by the rival,
will fret.
All the town will laugh, and with it the wench and her
beau.
Women are lacking in pity for those dejected and low,
Changeable like a child, like winds that blow in the
spring.
Give her nothing, and soon she'll find other farthings
that ring.
Promise her something again, and soon she'll be back in
your arms,
For her purse when it's full will spark her hopes and her
charms.
Money will call her hither, she'll fly to you, ousting the
other.
So with cunning and guile one cheater will swindle
another.
Purses lure any wench, as morsels of fowl or of meat
Lure and trap the birds whenever they're eager to eat.
Once she's received her price, into such an oath she will
burst:
"Leave you? Never, my dear, unless you abandon me
first."

Cum dederis nummum, iurabit te fore summum,
Tunc finget lacrimas partesque dabit tibi primas.
"Alter plura licet michi det, te plus amo" dicet,
Munus ut extricet et totum prodiga siccet.
Nam sua custodit, te nescia parcere rodit,
Tardantemque fodit, nisi des cito, quod volet, odit.
Cumque miser tua das, non querit, dum sibi tradas,
Unde hoc corrodas vel egens quo denique vadas.

7. Iussa lupanari meretrix

Iussa lupanari meretrix exire, parari
Provida vult ante, quamvis te sepe vocante.
Conponit vultum, meliorem dat sibi cultum,
Illinit unguento faciem, prodit pede lento.
Cum venit ingressa, residet spirans quasi fessa
Seque verecunde venisse refert aliunde,
Quamquam venit heri, simulans timuisse videri.
Cuius in adventum famulorum turba frequentum
Extendit leta cortinas atque tapeta.
Flagrat tota rosis et unguentis preciosis
Vestibus instrata domus, ut sit ei mage grata.
Omnia magnifice disponis pro meretrice,
Maiori cura cocus aptat fercula plura.
Que quasi morosa, quasi comis, deliciosa

Once you have given her coin she'll vow you're a hero
and true,
Then she will feign many tears and make a star actor of
you.
"Johnny was freer with gifts, but I love only you," she
will cry.
Thus she may gain still more and, prodigal, milk you all
dry.
Her possessions she guards, but merciless she will divest
you,
Egging you on, and unless you give with speed, she'll
detest you.
Hand her all that you own, but she'll never ask while
you're giving
Whence you acquired this much and, stripped, how now
you'll be living.

7. *The Wench*   (Hugh of Orléans)

When asked to leave the brothel, the wench is bent on
stalling,
She shrewdly makes her toilet, despite your frequent
calling,
She makes herself attractive, puts rouge upon her face,
Applies enough perfume and comes with measured pace.
On entering she sighs like one who's almost dead,
"From other places," shyly she says, "I just have sped,"
Pretending apprehension, though here since yesterday.
When she arrives, the servants in throngs and spirits gay
And happiness spread rugs and curtains in the room,
Which bears the scent of roses, is fragrant of perfume;
The house is decked with hangings that she may like it
well
And all these preparations may cast a magic spell.
With greatest care the cook prepares a host of dishes.
She samples, tastes, and licks these dishes so delicious,

241

Singula percurrit, degustat, pauca ligurrit.
Servit tota domus. Cum vina dat optima promus,
Sorbillat paullum, vix adprecians ea naulum.
Tecum nocte cubat quasi virgo, que modo nubat,
Clamat, dum scandis, quia res nimis est tibi grandis,
Anxia cum lite iurat non posse pati te;
Cumque gemens plorat, aditum stringendo minorat;
Qui si sit patulus, vix inpleat hunc bene mulus.
Cras ubi dimittis, obnubit timpora vittis,
Ne quis noscat eam, dum transvolat illa plateam.

Cum domus exilis habet hanc, casa sordida, vilis,
Tunc sibi de rivo potum petit. In lare privo
Inplent lactuce festiva fercula luce
Aut olus aut fungi. Bene si quando volet ungi,
Tunc emit exta bovis sacianda cadavere quovis
Vel capre vel ovis pecudumve pedes tribus ovis;
Vel panis duri calefacto frustula iuri
Frangens infercit, alia cui nocte pepercit.
Vilia tunc villa, que fece fluunt, emit illa;
Fraude bacetigeri ne quid valeat retineri,
In virga numerum designat uterque dierum.
Venditor et villi metretas conputat illi
Pro quadrante decem prebens ad prandia fecem.
Tunc si scurra pedes pede nudo pulsat ad edes,
Mimus sive calo vel suetus ludere talo,
Pene rigente malo celer hostia frangere palo
Leno discinctus, cicius te mittitur intus.

Some more, some less, now peevish and now in humor
fine;
All serve, and when the butler brings in the choicest
wine,
She sips but finds that hardly it's worth her while; in bed
With you she acts like any virgin but newly wed,
Laments, as you ascend, about your giant thing,
And flattened by your weight, she sighs: "I'm suffering!"
With plaint she pulls together, all taut and tense, alack!
What once a mule could enter is now a tiny crack.
And when she leaves next day, her head is draped in
veils,
That no one there will know her as down the street she
sails.

When now her shoddy place, in filth and wrapped in
gloom,
Opens, she drinks of river, and in the living room
She feasts on "festive" food of lettuce by the plate,
Of cabbage and of mushrooms. Or if she'd gain more
weight,
She buys an ox's entrails, she buys cadaver too
Of goat or sheep or cattle—three penny's worth will do;
Some crusts of bread she softens in soups she'd put away,
And warms the whole concoction for yet another day.
Poor wine that's rich in dregs she buys for very little,
But lest the taverner should cheat her of a tittle,
Both he and she mark notches for every day on wood,
Then he doles out for her the wine that's less than good.
A farthing brings her dregs to last for ten such meals.
But when a barefoot clown would kick her door with
heels,
A juggler, stableboy or gamester from a pub,
A porter lewd who'd shatter her portal with a club—
She'll welcome him unquestioned, and that with extra
speed.

243

Plus habet inde pedes quam Peleus aut Diomedes
Nobiliorve Pelops, ita currit ad hostia velox.
Ad vocem lixe properat metuens ea rixe,
Turpes et incompta post scurram currere prompta.
Quelibet inmunda loca poscat, non pudibunda,
Spe levis argenti stabulo caput abdet olenti.
Quolibet inpelli levis ibit amore lucelli.
Sicut apis melli semel heret dura revelli,
Sic volat ad munus meretrix, quod scurra dat unus;
Quo semel accepto cuivis se vendet inepto.

He's nimbler too than Peleus or even Diomede,
Or Pelops, nobler still. To open doors she hurries,
She fears an altercation as toward his voice she scurries,
Unkempt and ugly, fawning upon the shameless scamp,
She's unabashed and sordid, to please the filthy tramp;
In hope of coins she hides her head in foulest stall.
For love of paltry gain she's quick to give her all.
As bees will cling to honey and can't be torn from there,
Just so the wench will fly to gifts her "love" may bear.
Then, once she has the gift from him, she'll sell herself
                    to Jack or Jim.

1. Omnia tempus habent

1.

"Omnia tempus habent,"   et ego breve postulo tempus,
Ut possim paucos   presens tibi reddere versus;
Electo sacro,   presens in tegmine macro,
Virgineo more   non hec loquor absque rubore.

CHAPTER VII

𝕬𝖉𝖉𝖎𝖙𝖎𝖔𝖓𝖆𝖑 𝕻𝖔𝖊𝖒𝖘 𝖔𝖋 𝖙𝖍𝖊 𝕬𝖗𝖈𝖍𝖎𝖕𝖔𝖊𝖙𝖆 𝖆𝖓𝖉 𝖂𝖆𝖑𝖙𝖍𝖊𝖗 𝖔𝖋 𝕮𝖍𝖆̂𝖙𝖎𝖑𝖑𝖔𝖓

THE ARCHIPOETA and Walther of Châtillon and their poems are discussed in the Introduction (pp. 28 ff.); the two poets are also represented earlier in this collection (the Archipoeta in Chapter 1, poem 2, Walther in Chapter IV, poem 2). Here again the Archipoeta is revealed as the typical sinning, begging, cajoling vagabond, but also as a poet of great ability and resourcefulness. As for Walther, poem 5 shows him in the unusual role of a father who looks upon his infant daughter (legitimate or not) as a potential source of comfort and support in his old age (as to whether such a poem can be interpreted biographically or not, see the Commentary, p. 293). In poems 6 and 7 Walther waxes bitter about deterioration and degeneration in the Church administration and does not hesitate to blame the upper clergy for the bad conditions. These poems illustrate the sharp satire against church dignitaries which Walther cultivated as a special genre; this satire has scarcely an equal before the Protestant Reformation.

1. First Request   (Archipoeta)

1.

Everything has its time,   I beg you for only a little,
Only enough to present you   with verses a few that
I've made.
Newly Elected, 't is you   I address in garments all
tattered,
Blushing of cheek and abashed,   like a maiden still
adolescent.

2.

Vive, vir immense!   Tibi concedit regimen se,
Consilio cuius regitur   validaque manu ius;
Pontificum flos es,   et maximus inter eos es.
Incolumis vivas,   plus Nestore consilii vas!

3.

Vir pie, vir iuste,   precor, ut moveam precibus te,
Vir racione vigens,   dat honorem tota tibi gens,
Amplecti minimos   magni solet esse viri mos:
Cor miseris flecte,   quoniam probitas decet hec te!

4.

Pauperie plenos   solita pietate fove nos
Et Transmontanos,   vir Transmontane, iuva nos!
Nulla michi certe   de vita spes nisi per te.

5.

Frigore sive fame   tolletur spiritus a me,
Asperitas brume necat   horriferumque gelu me,
Continuam tussim pacior,   tanquam tisicus sim,
Sencio per pulsum,   quod non a morte procul sum.

6.

Esse probant inopes   nos corpore cum reliquo pes;
Unde verecundo vultu   tibi verba precun-do,
In tali veste   non sto sine fronte penes te:
Liber ab interitu   sis et memor esto mei tu!

2.

Hail, all hail, O lord,   it is you who govern our city,
You whose powerful hand   with its wisdom shelters
                    the law.
You are the flower of priests,   yes, you are the greatest
                    among them,
Long may you live and well,   far wiser than Nestor
                    himself.

3.

Dutiful man and just,   I pray, let prayers beseech you,
Scion of reason, O hear me,   to you we proffer respect.
Mightiness always has offered   the humble love and
                    protection,
Open your heart to the poor: such virtuousness will
                    befit you.

4.

Show us your wonted mercy,   O lord, for we are the
                    paupers,
Render assistance to me—   one transmontane to
                    another!
Hope shines fitful for me,   what's left is harbored in
                    you.

5.

Cold and famine harass me,   in spirit I'm sadly
                    dejected,
Winter's harshness besets me   with all its terrible ice.
Coughing racks me with pain,   and perhaps it's a
                    touch of consumption.
Feeling my pulse, I know,   death is approaching in
                    haste.

6.

Feet like body reveal   that I haven't a sou in my pocket,
Wherefore in shame I accost you,   confessing my
                    humiliation.
Clad in a derelict's garb   I stand embarrassed before
                    you,
May misfortune ignore you,   and, Sire, be you mindful
                    of me!

2. Fama tuba dante sonum

1.

Fama tuba dante sonum
Excitata vox preconum
Clamat viris regionum
Advenire virum bonum,
Patrem pacis et patronum,
Cui Vienna parat tronum
Multitudo marchionum.
Turba strepens istrionum
Iam conformat tono tonum.
Genus omne balatronum
Intrat ante diem nonum,
Quisquis sperat grande donum.
Ego caput fero pronum,
Tanquam frater sim latronum,
Reus, inops racionum,
Sensus egens et sermonum.

2.

Nomen vatis vel personam
Manifeste non exponam,
Sed quem fuga fecit Ionam,
Per figuram satis bonam
Ione nomen ei ponam.

3.

Lacrimarum fluit rivus,
Quas effundo fugitivus
Intra cetum semivivus,
Tuus quondam adoptivus.
Sed pluralis genitivus,
Nequam nimis et lascivus,
Michi factus est nocivus.

2. Jonah's Confession (Archipoeta)

1.

Rumor, with its trumpet blowing
Mid the heralds' voices glowing
Tells the people far and wide
That a virtuous man has nighed,
Friend of peace and champion;
In Vienne there is a throne
Which for him the peers prepare.
Crowds of players rend the air,
Making ready tune on tune,
Many kinds of jugglers soon
Enter, waiting not a week.
Largess they and presents seek.
I alone walk bowed in grief,
Like the brother of a thief,
Guilty, handicapped in thought,
Robbed of feeling, speech and aught.

2.

But this poet's self and name
I'll not publicly proclaim.
Just like Jonah did he flee.
This suggests a simile,
So I'll call him Jonah too.

3.

Tears my eyes in moisture steep
Which as exile I must weep
In the whale and half undone,
Formerly your foster-son.
But my sex-urge very devious,
Often evil and lascivious,
Made a noxious man of me.

4.

Voluptate volens frui
Conparabar brute sui
Nec cum sancto sanctus fui.
Unde timens iram tui,
Sicut Ionas dei sui,
Fugam petens fuga rui.

5.

Ionam deprehensum sorte,
Reum tempestatis orte,
Condempnatum a cohorte
Mox absorbent ceti porte.
Sic et ego dignus morte
Prave vivens et distorte,
Cuius carnes sunt absorte,
Sed cor manet adhuc forte.
Reus tibi vereor te
Miserturum michi forte.

6.

Ecce Ionas tuus plorat,
Culpam suam non ignorat,
Pro qua cetus eum vorat,
Veniam vult et implorat,
Ut a peste, qua laborat,
Solvas eum, quem honorat,
Tremit, colit et adorat.

7.

Si remittas hunc reatum
Et si ceto des mandatum,
Cetus, cuius os est latum,
More suo dans hiatum
Vomet vatem decalvatum
Et ad portum destinatum
Feret fame tenuatum,
Ut sit rursus vates vatum
Scribens opus tibi gratum.

4.

Looking for a happy time,
I was like a brutal swine,
Holy I did not appear.
Now your wrath I hold in fear,
Just as Jonah did his Lord's,
So I fled and minced no words.

5.

Jonah, who was caught by fate,
Blamed for storms that don't abate,
Jonah, by men's curses followed,
Promptly by a whale was swallowed.
So I, who deserve to die,
Whose base life was but a lie,
Flesh of whom is all devoured,
But whose courage is not lowered,
Guiltily your wrath I dread.
Will you pity me instead?

6.

See, your Jonah weeps the more
Since his guilt he can't ignore.
Thus the whale makes him its meat,
He seeks pardon, would entreat
That from plague which he abhors
You he loves, fears and adores
May release and free him soon.

7.

If me, sinner, you'll unhand,
Will the Jonah-whale command,
Then, endowed with spacious jaw,
It will open wide its maw,
Spew the poet bald of pate
Out before some stated gate,
Weak with hunger—you might know it—,
Then once more this poet's poet
Will write verse that you'll call fine.

Te divine mentis fatum
Ad hoc iussit esse natum,
Ut decore probitatum
Et exemplis largitatum
Reparares mundi statum.
8.
Hunc reatum si remittas,
Inter enses et sagittas
Tutus ibo, quo me mittas,
Hederarum ferens vittas.
9.
Non timebo Ninivitas
Neque gentes infronitas.
Vincam vita patrum vitas
Vitans ea, que tu vitas,
Poetrias inauditas
Scribam tibi, si me ditas.
10.
Ut iam loquar manifeste,
Paupertatis premor peste
Stultus ego, qui penes te
Nummis, equis, victu, veste
Dies omnes duxi feste,
Nunc insanus plus Oreste
Male vivens et moleste,
Trutannizans inhoneste
Omne festum duco meste.
Res non eget ista teste.
11.
Pacis auctor, ultor litis,
Esto vati tuo mitis
Neque credas imperitis!
Genitivis iam sopitis
Sanccior sum heremitis.
Quicquid in me malum scitis,
Amputabo, si velitis.
Ne nos apprehendat sitis,
Ero palmes et tu vitis.

Since your intellect's divine,
Fate decreed you're born for this:
Worthiest in dignity,
Free in generosity,
You brought order back to earth.

8.

If my sin you will forgive,
Twixt the swords and darts I'll live
Safely, going where you send me,
With the ivy to attend me.

9.

Ninivites I shall not dread,
Nor the folk to folly bred.
Saint of saints I strive to be,
Fleeing evils that you flee.
Poetry invaluable
You'll get if you're charitable.

10.

Frankly I will make confession,
Poverty is my oppression.
Fool I who, when in your care,
Had coin, horses, clothes and fare.
Every day a feast I had,
Now I'm like Orestes—mad.
Living badly—sad my plight—,
I am like a parasite,
Parties make me sad and tense.
This requires no evidence.

11.

Judge and author of the peace,
Let your wrath against me cease.
Don't believe the stupid guild!
Since my amorous urge is stilled,
I'll be purer than recluses.
Evil of which one accuses
Me, I'll pluck if you are willing,
That my thirst may need no stilling,
I'll the vine be, you the branches.

3. Nocte quadam sabbati

1.

Nocte quadam sabbati   somno iam refectus,
Cum michi fastidio   factus esset lectus,
Signo crucis muniens   frontem, vultum, pectus
Indui me vestibus,   quibus eram tectus.

2.

Sic dum nec accumberem   neque starem rectus,
Tantus odor naribus   meis est iniectus,
Quantum nunquam protulit   spica nardi nec thus
Neque liquor balsami   recens et electus.

3.

Ortus erat lucifer,   stella matutina,
Cum perfusus undique   luce repentina
Sum raptus ad ethera   quadam vi divina.
Ubi deus raptor est,   dulcis est rapina.

4.

Repente sub pedibus   hunc relinquo mundum
Et in orbem videor   ingredi secundum,
Cuius admirabile   lumen et iocundum
Non valet exprimere   verbis os facundum.

5.

Non est ibi gemitus   neque vox dolentis,
Ubi sanctus populus   inmortalis gentis
Liber a periculis,   tutus a tormentis
Pace summa fruitur   et quiete mentis.

6.

Ibi pulchritudinem   vidi domus dei,
Ipsum tamen oculi   non videre mei.
Nam divine tantus est   splendor faciei,
Quod mirantur angeli,   qui ministrant ei.

3. *Vision*   (Archipoeta)

1.

On a certain Sabbath morn,   well refreshed by sleep,
Through with rest, I was disposed   out of bed to leap,
Strengthening my brow and face   breast and all I
                crossed,
Then put on my clothes that I   on the bed had tossed.

2.

While I neither lay in bed   nor stood up erect,
Fragrance sweet arose, it seemed   nostrils to affect.
Poignant spikenard, incense sharp   never to me came
With such scent; of balsam oil   I can say the same.

3.

Lucifer, the morning star,   had ascended bright,
When I was surrounded by   sudden brilliant light.
To the ether I was snatched   by God's power deft.
Snatching done by God Himself   is a pleasant theft.

4.

Suddenly beneath my feet   I desert the earth,
Seeming then to come into   other world and berth,
Whose irradiant, joyful light   shines upon the blest
With a beauty that no tongue   ever has expressed.

5.

Here no sighing can be heard,   neither grief nor strife,
Where the folk of holy state,   with immortal life,
Never knowing danger nor   spirits that torment,
Relish their eternal peace   with their minds' content.

6.

There His beauteous abode   —God's I saw unfold,
But the Lord's own countenance   could I not behold,
So resplendent is His face   wonderful to limn:
Even angels with amaze   minister to Him.

7.

Hic nec Aristotilem   vidi nec Homerum,
Tamen de sentenciis   nominum et rerum,
De natura generum   atque specierum
Magnus michi protulit   Augustinus verum.

8.

Post hec ad archangelum   loquens Michaelem,
Qui regit per angelos   populum fidelem,
Ab eo sum monitus,   ut secreta celem
Et celi consilia   nemini revelem.

9.

Unde quamvis cernerem   de futuris multa,
Que sunt intellectibus   hominum sepulta,
Celi tamen prodere   vereor occulta.
Tu vero ne timeas,   presul, sed exulta!

10.

Tibi deputatus est   unus angelorum,
Super omnes alios   os habens decorum,
Sicut tu virtutibus   operum clarorum
Meritis preradias   omnium proborum.

11.

Huius ope prelia   te vicisse scias,
Ut des deo gloriam   nec superbus fias!
Tui dux itineris   est per omnes vias,
Pro tuis excessibus   preces fundens pias.

12.

Per hunc regnum Siculum   fiet tui iuris,
Ad radicem arboris   ponitur securis.
Tyrannis extollitur   et est sine curis,
Sed eius interitus   venit instar furis.

13.

Nolo tibi denique   nimium blandiri
Neque meo domino   blandiens mentiri.
Nemo potest adeo   mundus inveniri,
Ut sit sine macula   mens et actus viri.

7.

Neither Artistotle nor   Homer did I spy,
But ideas and things, how they   came about, and why,
Genera and species too,   what they are forsooth,
These St. Augustine explained,   speaking naught but
      truth.

8.

Angel Michael too I saw   long to him I spoke,
Who through lower angels rules   faithful Christian
      folk.
Solemnly he warned me thus: "Secrets you'll conceal,
Heaven's counsel never to   mortal man reveal."

9.

Although many thus I saw   things of future date
Which our human intellect   ne'er will penetrate,
Yet I'm fearful to expose   what is called occult.
You alone, O archbishop,   fear not, but exult!

10.

There's an angel who as your   guardian is assigned,
He's most beautiful of all   ever one could find,
So in virtue, kindness, works   greatly you surpass
Charities of other men   heedless what their class.

11.

Through this angel's succor you   many a battle won,
Praise give unto God, by pride   never be undone!
Let your angel lead the way,   as you now proceed,
For your welfare he will pray,   duly intercede.

12.

Through this angel Sicily   will be yours to boot,
Soon the axe will fell the tree   extirpate the root.
Tyranny will raise its head,   show nor care nor grief,
But decay will conquer it   like a prowling thief.

13.

Yet I would not, noble lord,   flatter you too much,
Nor you, lord and master, with   lying praises touch.
No man here in all the world   can so pure we find
That he bears no flaw in aught: action, conduct, mind.

14.

Ille sanctus inclitus,   gemma sacerdotum,
Cuius nomen omnibus   reor esse notum,
Qui suis miraculis   replet orbem totum,
Se dicit adversum te   nimis esse motum.

15.

Cumque vellet conqueri   de te coram deo,
Vix querelam distulit   flexus fletu meo;
Flebam namque graviter,   sicut sepe fleo,
Lacrimis inducias   postulans ab eo.

16.

Fluebant ab oculis   lacrimarum rivi,
Et quia compescere   lacrimas nequivi,
De terra ridencium   lacrimans exivi,
Inventus in lectulo   more semivivi.

17.

Precor ergo, domine,   flos presentis evi,
Ut ad sancti graciam   redeas in brevi.
Res eius diripiunt   quidam lupi sevi,
Quas tu restituere   verbo potes levi.

18.

Quamvis incessabilis   sarcina curarum
Mentem tuam distrahat   nec fatiget parum,
Scire tamen opus est,   quod sit deo carum,
Iuvare viriliter   res ecclesiarum.

19.

Fac ergo concordiam   sancto cum Martino,
Qui pro te multociens   me potavit vino!
Quod hec pax sit melior   quam cum Palatino,
Novit, quisquis agitur   spiritu divino.

14.

This distinguished man of God,   gem of the
                    consecrated,
Whose good name's well known to all,   widely
                    celebrated,
Who through wondrous works of love   charms each
                    race and age,
He says that he's wroth at you,   in a burning rage.

15.

When to God he 'gainst yourself   planned his
                    accusation,
Scarcely could I change his mind   with my
                    lamentation;
Bitter tears I shed the while,   as I often shed,
Hoping he'd postpone the case—   tearfully I pled.

16.

From my eyes in constant streams   flowed a teary
                    torrent,
And because I could not check   such a briny current,
Regions meant for laughing folk,   bathed in tears, I left,
Lying invalid in bed,   half of life bereft.

17.

Therefore, lord, I beg of you,   you our epoch's boon,
That to holy clemency   you restore him soon.
Stole from him his property   savage wolves and wild,
This restore to him by your   intercession mild.

18.

Although many pressing cares   in a bundle packed
Join to weary you with thoughts   which your mind
                    distract,
This though it is good to know: God will like it best
If we heartily promote   His church's interest.

19.

Make your peace as best you can   with St. Martin's
                    abbot,
Oft for you he gave me wine,   't was a pleasant habit!
Better is a peace with him   than with Palatine,
All know that if guided by   Spirit that's divine.

20.

Cum te vir sanctissimus   vellet accusare,
Vix eum prohibui   lacrimans amare.
Et quia sic volui   pro te laborare,
Debes michi magnum quid   in hoc festo dare.

21.

Tussis indeficiens   et defectus vocis
Cum ruinam nuncient   obitus velocis,
Circumdant me gemitus   in secretis locis,
Nec iam libet solitis   delectare iocis.

22.

Quamvis tamen moriar   et propinquem fini,
Et me fata terreant   obitus vicini,
Non possum diligere   nomen Palatini,
Per quem facta carior   est lagena vini.

23.

Afflixit iniuriis   populum et clerum.
Sed de tot iniuriis   diversarum rerum
Ego non conquererer,   ut iam loquar verum,
Nisi michi carius   venderetur merum.

24.

Ut tyrannis comitis   exponatur ipsi,
Tales versus facio,   quales nunquam scripsi.
Omne ve, quod legitur   in Apocalipsi,
Ferat, nisi liberet   vites ab eclipsi.

25.

Interim me dominus   iuxta psalmum David
Regit et in pascue   claustro collocavit.
Hic michi, non aliis   vinum habundavit;
Abbas bonus pastor est   et me bene pavit.

20.

When 'gainst you this holy man   made his accusation,
I could scarcely check him with   bitter lamentation,
And since I on your behalf   labored willingly,
At this festive time you should   give a gift to me.

21.

Failing voice and constant cough   never give me peace,
Show that it will not be long   till my prompt decease.
Therefore I must sigh and hide,   fleeing from the sun,
Now I find no pleasure in   wonted jest and fun.

22.

Though I have to die forthwith   as I near the end,
Though the perils that I face   constant terror lend,
Yet I have no love for him,   lord Count Palatine,
Who has made the price go up   for a jug of wine.

23.

Common folk and clergy he   harmed, or even worse,
But of such injustice in   matters quite diverse
I would not complain at all,   save, the truth to tell,
That he's raised the price of wine   which to me he'd
                    sell.

24.

That his tyranny be now   everywhere exposed,
I shall write such verse as I   never have composed.
All the woes we read about,   told in Revelation,
May he suffer if he dooms   vines to decimation!

25.

Meanwhile God would guide me well,   David's psalm
                has said,
In the convent cell to fresh   pastures I am led,
Where the wine flows free for me,   not for any other;
Abbot, you my shepherd good,   fed me like a brother.

4. Presul urbis Agripine

Presul urbis Agripine,
Qui rigorem discipline
　　Bonitate temperas,
Nichil agens indiscrete,
Ne sit fama mendax de te,
　　Vita famam superas.

5. Verna redit temperies

1.

Verna redit temperies
Prata depingens floribus,
Telluris superficies
Nostris arridet moribus,
Quibus amor est requies,
Cybus esurientibus.

2.

Duo quasi contraria
Miscent vires effectuum,
Augendo seminaria
Reddit natura mutuum,
Ex discordi concordia
Prodit fetura fetuum.

3.

Letentur ergo ceteri,
Quibus Cupido faverit,
Sed cum de plaga veteri
Male michi contigerit,
Vita solius miseri
Amore quassa deperit.

4. In Praise of Archbishop
Reinald von Dassel   (Archipoeta)

Ruler of Cologne, the town,
Discipline brings you renown,
Tempered, archbishop, with kindness.
What you do, you do discreetly,
Hence your reputation meetly
Casts a luster like your life.

5. My Daughter   (Walther of Châtillon)

1.

These days mark springtime's glad rebirth,
They paint the meadows bright with flowers,
The outer face of all the earth
Its friendliness upon us showers;
Love is to us a restful mood,
While for the famished it is food.

2.

The power of substances will blend,
Though opposites they seem to be;
E'er stronger in its fertile trend,
Nature pays back unselfishly.
Discordant concord can create
New creatures freshly animate.

3.

Let then the other folk be glad
Whom Cupid favors in his way,
But cruel buffets make me sad
That visited me yesterday.
My life alone with grief is battered
And doomed, because my love is shattered.

4.

Ille nefastus merito
Dies vocari debuit,
Qui sub nature debito
Natam michi constituit,
Dies, qui me tam subito
Relativum instituit.

5.

Cresce tamen, puellula,
Patris futura baculus,
In senectute querula,
Dum caligabit oculus,
Mente ministrans sedula
Plus proderis quam masculus.

6. Licet eger cum egrotis

1.

Licet eger cum egrotis
Et ignotus cum ignotis,
Fungar tamen vice cotis,
Ius usurpans sacerdotis.
Flete, Syon filie!
Presides ecclesie
Imitantur hodie
Christum a remotis.

2.

Si privata degens vita
Vel sacerdos vel levita
Sibi dari vult petita
Ac incedit via trita,
Previa fit paccio
Symonis auspicio,
Cui succedit dacio,
Et sic fit Giezita.

4.

That day seemed cursed to me with reason,
Abusing me like any churl,
Which, in its duly proper season,
Bestowed on me a baby girl—
A sudden change without ado
Made me a father fresh and new.

5.

O daughter, grow up none the less,
Your father's staff to be some day
In his old age's peevish stress
When once his sight has dimmed for ay!
't is then you'll be his help and joy
Far more than ever would a boy.

6. *Complaint against the Upper Clergy*
(Walther of Châtillon)

1.

Though I'm sick 'mongst those who ail,
Stranger in a foreign pale,
Like a whetstone I would be,
Claiming priestly rights for me.
Zion's daughters, weep, I say!
Princes of the church today
Perspicaciously essay
To be Antichrist.

2.

Should they who no office fill,
Priest or Levite, if you will,
Hope to benefit by gain,
On the wellworn paths remain,
Firstly they'll conclude a pact,
Simony 't is called in fact,
Then a bribery they enact,
Thus they join the Gehazites.

3.

Iacet ordo clericalis
In respectu laicalis,
Sponsa Christi fit mercalis,
Generosa generalis;
Veneunt altaria,
Venit eucharistia,
Cum sit nugatoria
Gracia venalis.

4.

Donum Dei non donatur,
Nisi gratis conferatur;
Quod qui vendit vel mercatur,
Lepra Syri vulneratur.
Quem sic ambit ambitus,
Idolorum servitus,
Templo sancti Spiritus
Non compaginatur.

5.

In diebus iuventutis
Timent annos senectutis,
Ne fortuna destitutis
Desit eis splendor cutis.
Et dum querunt medium,
Vergunt in contrarium,
Fallit enim vicium
Specie virtutis.

6.

Si quis tenet hunc tenorem,
Frustra dicit se pastorem
Nec se regit ut rectorem,
Renum mersus in ardorem.
Hec est enim alia
Sanguisuge filia,
Quam venalis curia
Duxit in uxorem.

3.

Low have sunk the clericals
In the eyes of laicals,
Christ's betrothed grows meretricious,
Noble born and yet she's vicious;
Altars are for lucre sold,
E'en the Host now goes for gold,
Since all mercy's false and cold
When it's won through bribes.

4.

Gifts of God are ne'er conferred
If for free they're not incurred;
Who would sell or trade them, he
Suffers Gehazi's leprosy.
But who's driven to it by greed
(On it idol-mongers feed),
Him the Holy Ghost won't lead
To his sacred temple.

5.

In their early youthful stage
They already fear old age,
Lest when fortune wealth disperse
Their complexion will get worse.
While they seek a middle groove
In a different course they move;
Vice will often try to prove
That it's really virtue.

6.

If it's this at which you've aimed,
Pastor you can not be named,
Neither will you act as guide
While in passion you abide.
Lechery's a sister too
Of that base bloodsucking shrew
Whom the venal Curia drew
To its heart as wife.

7.

Ut iam loquar inamenum,
Sanctum crisma datur venum,
Iuvenantur corda senum
Nec refrenant motus renum.
Senes et decrepiti
Quasi modo geniti
Nectaris illiciti
Hauriunt venenum.

8.

Ergo nemo vivit purus,
Castitatis perit murus,
Commendatur Epicurus
Nec spectatur moriturus.
Grata sunt convivia;
Auro vel pecunia
Cuncta facit pervia
Pontifex futurus.

7. Versa est in luctum

1.

Versa est in luctum
Cythara Waltheri,
Non quia se ductum
Extra gregem cleri
Vel eiectum doleat
Aut abiecti lugeat
Vilitatem morbi,
Sed quia considerat,
Quod finis accelerat
Improvisus orbi.
    Libet intueri
    Iudices ecclesie,
    Quorum status hodie
    Peior est quam heri.

7.

Listen to this ugly tale:
Holy chrism's now for sale,
Old men's hearts are young again
As they give their lust full rein.
Old men and debilitated,
Just as though rejuvenated,
Quaff forbidden nectar sated
With the deadly poison.

8.

None of them is pure at all,
Down comes chastity's frail wall,
Epicurus too is praised,
No one now by death is fazed.
Feasts bring days of mirth and glee;
Bishop do you aim to be?
Then resort to bribery,
That makes all roads open.

7. *The End of the World*   (Walther of Châtillon)

1.

Now to plaints addicted,
Walther's harp must sing,
Not that he's evicted
From the clergy's ring,
Which might cause his grief to grow,
Not that illness lays him low,
Noisome that it's been,
But because he sees in fear
That the end for all draws near,
Wholly unforeseen.
  We may well survey
  Churchmen charged with legislation,
  Worse has grown their reputation
  E'en since yesterday.

2.

Umbra cum videmus
Valles operiri,
Proximo debemus
Noctem experiri;
Sed cum montes videris
Et colles cum ceteris
Rebus obscurari,
Nec fallis nec falleris,
Si mundo tunc asseris
Noctem dominari.
   Libet intueri
   Iudices ecclesie,
   Quorum status hodie
   Peior est quam heri.

3.

Per convalles nota
Laicos exleges,
Notos turpi nota
Principes et reges,
Quos pari iudicio
Luxus et ambicio
Quasi nox obscurat,
Quos celestis ulcio
Bisacuto gladio
Perdere maturat.
   Libet intueri
   Iudices ecclesie,
   Quorum status hodie
   Peior est quam heri.

4.

Restat, ut per montes
Figurate notes
Scripturarum fontes:
Christi sacerdotes
Colles dicti mystice,
Eo quod in vertice
Syon constituti

2.

When the shadows grow,
Darkening the vales,
We are bound to know:
Night will shroud all trails;
Then when later you've discovered
Mountains, hills and all things covered
In obscurity,
You'll not err but speak aright
If you say that now the night
Rules us utterly.
    We may well survey
    Churchmen charged with legislation,
    Worse has grown their reputation
    E'en since yesterday.

3.

Through the valleys, lo!
Lawless laymen pace,
Kings and princes go,
All in deep disgrace,
Whom in uniform condition
Luxury and high ambition
Darken like the night,
Whom the vengeance of the Lord,
Armed with two-edged battle-sword,
To the death would fight.
    We may well survey
    Churchmen charged with legislation,
    Worse has grown their reputation
    E'en since yesterday.

4.

Understand: the mountains
Are a figure for
Holy Scripture's fountains:
So the priests of Christ
Are the hills in mystic speech,
Since on Zion's highest reach,
Where they throne in state,

Mundo sunt pro speculo,
Si legis oraculo
Vellent non abuti.
  Libet intueri
  Iudices ecclesie,
  Quorum status hodie
  Peior est quam heri.
     5.
Iubent nostri colles
Dari cunctis fenum
Et preferri molles
Sanctitati senum;
Fit hereditarium
Dei sanctuarium,
Et ad Christi dotes
Preponuntur hodie
Expertes sciencie
Presulum nepotes.
  Si rem bene notes,
  Succedunt in vicium
  Et in beneficium
  Terreni nepotes.
     6.
Veniat in brevi,
Iesu bone deus,
Finis huius evi,
Annus iubileus!
Moriar, ne videam
Antichristi frameam,
Cuius precessores
Iam non sani dogmatis
Stant in monte crismatis
Censuum censores.
  Si rem bene notes,
  Succedunt in vicium
  Et in beneficium
  Terreni nepotes.

They are models pure as gold
For us all, if they'll uphold
Law no man should hate.
   We may well survey
   Churchmen charged with legislation,
   Worse has grown their reputation
   E'en since yesterday.

5.

Now our hills forsooth
Would give all men hay,
They'd prefer the youth,
Age they would gainsay;
Would give heaven's sanctity
Full heritability,
While priests' relatives
In their lack of wisdom's power
Would enjoy this very hour
Gifts bestowed by Christ.
   Please to note this well:
   Sins and benefices too
   Children will inherit who
   On this earth may dwell.

6.

Let the world's decay,
Dear Lord Jesus Christ,
Come without delay
In this jubilee!
I would rather die than see
Antichrist's lance lancing me.
His allies—beware!—
Teaching dogmas counterfeit
Stand upon Mount Olivet,
Taking tribute there.
   Please to note this well:
   Sins and benefices too
   Children will inherit who
   On this earth may dwell.

Previous English Translations of Poems in This Volume

Prelude

O Fortuna. Whicher, *The Goliard Poets,* p. 262.

Chapter I

Poem 1: *Cum in orbem universum.* Symonds, *Wine, Women, and Song,* p. 46; Lindsay, *Medieval Latin Poets,* pp. 191 ff.; Whicher, pp. 272 ff.

Symonds and Whicher do not follow the now accepted sequence of strophes.

Poem 2: *Estuans intrinsecus.* Symonds, p. 59; Waddell,* pp. 182 ff. (also her *Wandering Scholars,* pp. 155 ff.); Lindsay, pp. 166 ff.; Whicher, pp. 106 ff.

Only Lindsay gives the twenty-five strophes in correct sequence.

Poem 3: *Pontificum spuma.* Whicher, p. 80.

Poem 4: *Hoc indumentum.* Whicher, p. 80.

Poem 6: *Exul ego clericus.* Symonds, p. 54; Lindsay, pp. 195 f.; Whicher, p. 224.

Poem 8: *Raptor mei pilei.* Whicher, p. 286.

Chapter II

Poem 1: *In taberna quando sumus.* Whicher, pp. 226 ff.

Poem 2: *Ego sum abbas.* Symonds, p. 161; Lindsay, pp. 199 f.

Poem 3: *Bacche, benevenias.* Lindsay, pp. 205 f.; Whicher, pp. 230 ff.

Poem 5: *Olim lacus colueram.* Symonds, pp. 157 f.; Lindsay, p. 207; Whicher, p. 250.

None follow the now accepted sequence of strophes.

* "Waddell" refers to the Penguin edition of *Medieval Latin Lyrics* unless otherwise noted.

CHAPTER III

Poem 1: *Levis exsurgit zephirus.* Waddell, p. 169; Allen, *The Romanesque Lyric* (tr. Jones), p. 290; Lindsay, pp. 120 f.; Whicher, p. 26.

Poem 2: *Iam, dulcis amica, venito.* Symonds, p. 15; Allen, p. 288 f.; Waddell, pp. 156 ff.; Lindsay, pp. 121 f.; Whicher, p. 24.

Poem 4: *Letabundus rediit.* Waddell, p. 226; Lindsay, pp. 219 f.; Whicher, pp. 172 ff.

Poem 5: *Ecce gratum.* Symonds, p. 74.

Poem 6: *Ver redit optatum.* Symonds, p. 67; Whicher, p. 202.

Poem 7: *Dum Diane vitrea.* Symonds, p. 95; Waddell, p. 276 (also in *Wandering Scholars*, pp. 148 f.); Lindsay, pp. 229 ff.; Whicher, p. 30.
    All add spurious strophes.

Poem 8: *Veris dulcis in tempore.* Symonds, p. 81; Lindsay, pp. 220 f.; Whicher, p. 210.

Poem 10: *Amor habet superos.* Whicher, pp. 166 ff.

Poem 11: *Lingua mendax et dolosa.* Symonds, p. 125; Whicher, pp. 182 ff.

Poem 12: *De pollicito.* Symonds, p. 82.

Poem 13: *Dulce solum.* Symonds, p. 134.

Poem 14: *Huc usque me miseram.* Symonds, p. 131; Lindsay, pp. 238 f.; Whicher, pp. 190 ff.

Poem 15: *Volo virum vivere.* Waddell, p. 240; Lindsay, pp. 231 f.

Poem 19: *Omittamus studia.* Symonds, p. 88; Waddell, p. 214; Lindsay, pp. 207 f.; Whicher, pp. 176 ff.

Poem 20: *Vacillantis trutine.* Whicher, p. 178.

Poem 21: *Si puer cum puellula.* Symonds, p. 115; Lindsay, p. 224.

Poem 22: *Veni, veni, venias.* Symonds, p. 111; Lindsay, p. 218.

Poem 23: *Stetit puella.* Waddell (*Wandering Scholars*), p. 207; Lindsay, pp. 221 f.; Whicher, p. 220.

Chapter IV

Poem 1: *Estivali sub fervore. Symonds,* p. 91.
Poem 3: *Vere dulci mediante.* Whicher, p. 214.
Poem 5: *Exiit diluculo.* Symonds, p. 91; Lindsay, p. 221;
Whicher, p. 194.

Chapter V

Poem 1: *Anni parte florida.* "R.S." in George Chapman's
Ouid's Banquet of Sence, London, 1595 (see Wright,
The Latin Poems . . . , pp. 363 ff.); Symonds (in part),
pp. 99 ff.; Lindsay (in part), pp. 136 ff.

Chapter VI

Poem 1: *Magnus cesar Otto.* Allen (in part), pp. 282 f.;
Lindsay, pp. 123 ff.
Poem 2: *Advertite, omnes populi.* Allen, pp. 275 f.; Lindsay, pp. 113 f.
Poem 3: *Mendosam quam cantilenam.* Allen, pp. 277 f.;
Lindsay, pp. 119 f.
Poem 4: *Est unus locus.* Allen, pp. 280 f.; Lindsay, pp. 114 f.
Poem 5: *O admirabile Veneris idolum.* Allen, p. 285.
Poem 6: *Quid luges, lirice.* Lindsay, pp. 176 ff.

Chapter VII

Poem 1: *Omnia tempus habent.* Whicher, p. 104.
Poem 2: *Fama tuba dante sonum.* Whicher, pp. 120 ff.
Poem 5: *Verna redit temperies.* Whicher, p. 130.
Poem 6: *Licet eger cum egrotis.* Whicher, pp. 132 ff.
Poem 7: *Versa est in luctum.* Whicher, pp. 136 ff.

Commentary

Prelude

The Wheel of Fortune (Carmina Burana—No. 17)

This song is, in a sense, the theme of the *Carmina Burana,* at least so far as the vagabond songs are concerned. The best illustration in the manuscript pictures it, and it is used by Orff as his prelude and is sung by the chorus.

Chapter I, *Poem 1.*

Song of the Vagabond Order (Carmina Burana— No. 219)

The poet here pretends that such an order exists, to which he facetiously assigns a place beside the ecclesiastical orders (they had increased greatly in number during the twelfth century). The language resembles that of the monastic rules, which are parodied. As described here, the new rules advocate a worldly life of carousing.

1, 1 (strophe 1, line 1) quotes and parodies Mark 16: 15: "And he said unto them: 'Go ye into all the world and preach the gospel to every creature.'" The *sacerdotes* are the priests, the *levitae* the deacons and sub-deacons.

2, 2 parodies I Thess. 5:21: "Prove all things; hold fast that which is good."

6 is incomplete in the manuscript.

8, 7 ff.: *Hordei mensura* could be either a tithe of grain for the priest or the barley water of the beneficed clergyman.

10, 8: Hasardhi, a personification of Chance (French *hasard*).

11, 5: *Hic et hec et hoc,* a play on the declension of the demonstrative.

12, 6: Decius, the god of gaming.

16 is a variation of a strophe from one of the poems of Walther of Châtillon.

16: 5–8: Matt. 25:32: "And he shall separate them one from another, as a shepherd divideth his sheep from the goats."

Poem 2.
Vagabond's Confession (Carmina Burana—No. 191)

This is found also in the Göttingen manuscript (philol. 170), and is in the Watenphul-Krefeld edition (No. 10). It was probably written in the autumn of 1163 for Reinald von Dassel. Originally, strophes 14–19 were missing; they were added later from another poem in which he explains why he will not write an epic on Emperor Frederick I. The title refers more to the form of the poem than to its contents. The poet seems to be contrite and repentent and acknowledges his excesses and sins; he vows to improve, asks for lenience, and craves absolution. In reality, however, he offers reasons for his sins and seeks to justify himself: as a vagabond, he must follow his own bent. An early melody is found in manuscript 490/491 of the Proske library, Regensburg, dating from 1557–1559. The first five strophes are used by Orff (No. 11) as baritone solo.

1, 3: Job 10: 1: "I will leave my complaint upon myself; I will speak in the bitterness of my soul."

1, 7: Job 13:25: "Wilt thou break a leaf driven to and fro? and wilt thou pursue the dry stubble?"

2, 1 f.: Matt. 7:24: "Therefore whosoever heareth these sayings of mine . . . I will liken him unto a wise man, which built his house upon a rock."

2, 5 ff.: Horace, *Epist.* I, 2, 42 f.: *Rusticus exspectat, dum defluat amnis; at ille / Labitur et labitur in omne volubilis aevum* ("the rustic waits for the current and is carried along").

3, 1 ff.: The similes of the ship and the bird are also biblical.

4, 4: Ps. 19:10.

5, 1: Matt. 7:14: ". . . and narrow is the way, which leadeth unto life, and few there be that find it."

5, 5 f.: II Tim. 3:4: "Traitors, heady, highminded, lovers of pleasure more than lovers of God."

6, 1: *Presul* is Reinald, archbishop of Cologne (see also 24, 1).

6, 7 f.: Matt. 5:28: "But I say unto you, That whosoever looketh on a woman to lust after her hath committed adultery with her already in his heart."

8, 3 ff.: Pavia, in northern Italy, had a reputation for immorality.

9, 1: Hippolytus defended his chastity against Phaedra, his stepmother, and thus gave up his life. Ovid, *Amores* II, 4, 32: *Illic Hippolytum pone, Priapus erit* ("put Hippolytus there, and he will be debauched").

9, 8: *Turris Ariciae* was the tower in which Diana hid Hippolytus from Jupiter's wrath. The nymph Aricia was the wife of Hippolytus.

11, 8: A reminiscence of the words of several masses for the dead.

12: See Ovid, *Amores* II, 10, 35 ff.: *At mihi contigat Veneris languescere motu, / Cum moriar* ("may I be in Venus' arms when I die"), which expresses a very similar wish applied to love. This and the following strophes, usually beginning *Mihi est propositum,* became a separate, inferior song, widely disseminated as a composition of "Walter Mapes." The music referred to above was meant for it.

12, 7: See Luke 18:13: "And the publican . . . smote upon his breast, saying, God be merciful to me, a sinner."

14, 1 f.: See Horace, *Epist.* II, 2, 77: *Scriptorum chorus omnis amat nemus et fugit urbem* ("writers like the grove and flee the city").

16, 1 f. and 17, 1 ff.: See I Cor. 7:7: "But every man hath his proper gift of God . . ."

19, 7: Phoebus Apollo is also the god of poetry and music.

20, 1 ff.: Prov. 18:17: "He that is first in his own cause seemeth just."

21, 3 ff.: John 8:7: "He that is without sin among you, let him first cast a stone at her."

22, 7 f.: I Sam. 16:7: ". . . for man looketh on outward appearance, but the Lord looketh on the heart."

22, 8: Jupiter (Jove) here is God.

23, 5 f.: I Pet. 2:2: "As newborn babes, desire the sincere milk of the word, that ye may grow thereby."

24, 1: Reinald von Dassel is addressed.

25, 1 ff.: The thought is expressed in *De mirabilibus mundi* falsely ascribed to Ovid, but is also in *Historia ecclesiastica* of Ordericus Vitalis (discovered by Paul Lehmann): *Parcere prostratis scit nobilis ira leonis. / Tu quoque fac simile, quisquis dominaris in orbe* ("The angry lion spares one who is down. Rulers, do the same").

Poems 3, 4.
Curses on the Bishop.
Dialog while Walking (Wilhelm Meyer—Nos. 2a, 2b)

These two epigrams by Hugh of Orléans, plus a third omitted here, might be considered a unit in three parts. But originally they probably concerned different gifts. The speakers in poem 4 are Hugh himself and a passerby. Hugh also wrote other epigrams on furless coats without linings.

Poem 5.
Bishop, Drink! (Wilhelm Meyer—No. 11)

Hugh advises a bishop not given to drinking that a good churchman must also be a stout drinker. The dig about his virility is a bold allusion to the prelate's reputation with women.

Poem 6.
A Plea for Clothing (Carmina Burana—No. 129)

This poem is a typical vagabond student's plea, far from home and impecunious, for clothing. Poverty has forced him to abandon his studies. Strophe 5 (N=*nomen nescio*, or the like) indicates that the song may be addressed at will to any likely patron, but Jacob Grimm erroneously thought the letter H was meant, and interpreted it as standing for *Herbipoleos*, genitive of Herbipolis, Würzburg. St. Martin is the saint of many churches, especially in France.

Poem 7.
Farewell to Swabia

This song was discovered and first published by J. Werner in *Beiträge zur Kunde der lateinischen Literatur des Mittelalters* (Aarau, 1905), pp. 134 f. The localization is interesting. Some think strophes 1–4 and 5–8 are separate songs, but the two parts are clearly related.

5, 8: Socrates was the philosopher par excellence.

6, 1: Luke 23:46: "Father, into thy hands I commend my spirit."

6, 7: Isa. 63:1: "Who is this that cometh from Edom, with dyed garments from Bozrah?" This is always thought to be a reference to Christ. Bozrah lies south of the Dead Sea.

8, 1: Paris is meant. *Denuo* may indicate that this is his second trip, but here we interpret it differently.

8, 7 f.: The mystic pearl is wisdom, see Matt. 13:45 f.: "Again, the kingdom of heaven is like unto a merchant man, seeking goodly pearls: Who, when he had found one pearl of great price, went and sold all that he had and bought it."

Poem 8.
Death to the Thief!

This song is from Wright, *The Latin Poems* . . . (pp. 75 f.). The humor of the poem lies in the discrepancy between the petty theft and the enormity of the execrations. Catullus wrote some comparable poems.

1, 7: Elysium is the home of the blessed in the Lower World.

1, 8: Lethe is the river of forgetfulness there.

2, 5: On the Book of Life, see Rev. 3:5 ff., 20:12 ff., and Ps. 69:28.

2, 7: Aeacus, a judge of the dead.

3, 5: Cerberus is the dog guarding the gates of hell.

3, 8: The Erinnys are the three Furies, of whom Alecto (4, 8) is one.

CHAPTER II, *Poem 1.*
Drinking (Carmina Burana—No. 196)

This song is used by Orff (No. 14) for a male chorus. A parody of various prayers is intended here: strophes 3–4 are based upon the Good Friday liturgy, 5–6 upon the Corpus Christi sequence, *Lauda, Sion, salvatorem* ("Zion praise the Savior"). Compare the last two lines of the poem with Ps. 69:28: "Let them be blotted out of the book of the living, and not be written with the righteous."

1, 6: Where drinks are cheap.

Poem 2.
The Abbot of Cockaigne (Carmina Burana—No. 222)

Used by Orff (No. 13) for baritone solo and male chorus. It is possibly aimed at some abbot. Since Cockaigne is a French concept, the first part of the song probably originated in France. The first six lines are in rhythmic prose. *Wafna,* from Middle High German *Wâfen* (weapons), is an exclamation of alarm.

Poem 3.
Song to Bacchus (Carmina Burana—No. 200)

Again, a parody of various prayers. The refrain was meant to be sung by the entire gathering of drinkers— the congregation.

Poem 4.
Roundelay

This song is not in the *Carmina Burana*. It was first published by H. Walther in *Mittelalterliche Handschriften,*

Festgabe für H. Degering (Leipzig, 1926), pp. 296 ff.
See Karl Langosch, *Vagantendichtung* (Berlin), p. 92.
It parodies a solemn meeting of conferees, religious or
secular. *honeste—modeste* in the last strophe remind
one of the Middle High German ideal of *diu mâze*
(moderation).

Poem 5.
Song of the Roasted Swan (*Carmina Burana*—No. 130)

Orff used this song (No. 12) for tenor solo and male
chorus. Swans were served like geese as delicacies in
the Middle Ages. Some editors arrange the strophes in
the order: 1, 3, 4, 2, 5, and in strophe 3 place line 2 before line 1. In 1, 1 some read *latus* ("I took care of my
body, preened my feathers"), instead of *lacus* ("I swam
in the lakes").

CHAPTER III, Poem 1.
A Maiden's Sighs in Springtime (Cambridge Songs—
No. 41)

This song was published by Karl Strecker in a special
edition of the *Monumenta Germaniae Historica* (Berlin,
1926), and by W. Bulst in the *Editiones Haidelbergenses*
(No. 17, 1950).

Poem 2.
Invitation to the Beloved (Cambridge Songs—No. 27)

Strophes 1–5 are sung by the lover. Strophe 6, sung by
the girl, is puzzling because it is in the perfect tense.
Of strophe 7 only four words are preserved. Strophe 8 is
still spoken by the girl, the last two strophes by the lover.
The reference to postponement in strophe 9 (*differre*)
is also puzzling. Perhaps the poem is more fragmentary
than it seems.

Poem 3.
To Springtime (*Carmina Burana*—No. 81)

This song of jubilation over the coming of spring, after

a long north European winter, strongly resembles numerous Middle High German songs. It is a dancing song —a song of the *tripudium* in which the dancers stamp three times at regular intervals—and love is not linked with it. Even the *anus, licet vetula* (old lady) appears in Walther von der Vogelweide (in his song, *Dô der sumer komen was*).

Poem 4.
The Coming of Spring (*Carmina Burana*—No. 74)

1, 7: Phoebus Apollo is the sun god.

2, 1: Jove stands for the heavens. Perhaps strophe 2 should follow strophe 4; or is the proper order: 1, 4, 3, 2, 5?

3: Dryads are tree nymphs, Oreads mountain nymphs, Satyrs woodland fauns. Tempe is a beautiful valley in Thessaly, sacred to Apollo.

Poem 5.
Joys of Springtime (*Carmina Burana*—No. 143)

Orff used this song (No. 5) as a chorus.

3, 7: Cypris refers to Venus, so called for her favorite island of Cyprus. Paris, the Trojan prince who kidnapped Helen, stands for lovers in general.

Poem 6.
Advice in Spring (*Carmina Burana*—No. 137)

Many such poems have a third strophe dealing with the singer's own beloved. In 1, 8, the manuscript has *carmen amenus* ("the song is pleasant"). Schumann changed this in the standard edition (I, 2, 230 f.).

Poem 7.
Sleep and Love (*Carmina Burana*—No. 62)

In the manuscript the poem has four additional strophes. Waddell, *Medieval Latin Lyrics* (pp. 264 ff.), uses 5 and

7, omitting 6 and 8. Lindsay (pp. 229 ff.) and Whicher (pp. 30 ff.) use all eight. In the standard edition, Schumann (I, 2, pp. 20 ff.) shows that 5–8 are all later spurious additions.

1 ff.: Diana's lamp is the moon, her brother's (Appollo's) is the sun.

With great artistry the poem describes sleep gradually overcoming the poet.

Poem 8.
Song of Love (Carmina Burana—No. 85)

1, 3: Juliana is an exotic name like many others in the vagabond poems.

Poem 9.
Bond of Love (Carmina Burana—No. 88a)

Astrology was a favorite pastime in the Middle Ages. Two additional strophes after strophe 2, and two more after strophe 4, were rejected by Schumann as spurious.

Poem 10.
Cecilia (Carmina Burana—No. 88)

8: This refers to five *lineae amoris* (steps to love) referred to as early as 350 A.D. in a commentary on the plays of Terence by Aelius Donatus. These steps are *visus* (seeing), *allocutio* (accosting), *tactus* (touching), *osculum sive suavium* (kissing), and *coitus* (see III, 16, strophe 2a).

Poem 11.
Pledge of Love (Carmina Burana—No. 117)

4: Jupiter's love adventure with Danae (or Dane) is told in Ovid, *Metamorphoses* II, 561 ff.

5: Phoebus Apollo had affairs with Daphne, Cassandra, Sibyl, and others. Among his sons were Aesculapius, Orpheus, and Phaethon. Mars and Venus deceived Vulcan. Romulus was the son of Mars and Rhea Silvia.

8, 3: Notice the change of beat to avoid hiatus, which would result from: *pectus, humeri et* . . . , but see 10, 3.

11: The Parthians, living southeast of the Caspian Sea, were famous as marksmen with the bow and arrow.

Poem 12.
Love's Sorrow (Carmina Burana—No. 171)

4, 3: Ceres was the goddess of harvests and grain.

Poem 13.
Deadly Love (Carmina Burana—No. 119)

In a manuscript in the municipal library of Chartres, France (223, s 13/14, fol. 66ᵛ), this song is well provided with neumes.

4, 2: Hybla, in Sicily, is praised by Ovid and Vergil for its honey, flowers, and thyme.

4, 4: Dodona was an oracle in Epirus; the rustling trees served as the voice.

Poem 14.
The Deserted Girl (Carmina Burana—No. 126)

This is one of the finest of the *carmina;* it bears comparison with Gretchen's song, "Meine Ruh ist hin" (in Goethe's *Faust*), and savors of Ovid.

Poem 15.
The Man's Wish (Carmina Burana—No. 178)

2, 11–12: Note the effective chiasmus and parallelism.

4, 4: On Hippolytus see note on I, 2, strophe 9, 1.

Poem 16.
Coronis (Carmina Burana—No. 72; Arundel—No. 10)

This poem is a sequence in form.

1b, 7: Dione is the mother of Venus, here used for Venus.

2a, 1 ff.: See note on III, 10.

Poem 17.

The Love of My Choice (Arundel—No. 28)

The wishes of a very fastidious lover are here expressed; he wants his lady not too young and not too old—but also not too chaste.

1, 11: The Sabine women were reputed to be chaste.

Poem 18.

Invective against Venus (Vatican Library— Vat. Lat. 4389)

This is one of the finest vagabond songs; the manner in which the theme is treated is unusual. The meter too is unconventional, as is the refrain.

4, 3: The son of Laertes was Odysseus. His comrades killed the cattle of the sun god Helios, whose daughter, Circe, Odysseus later frustrated after she turned his men into swine.

Poem 19.

Adieu to Studies (Carmina Burana—No. 75)

There are echoes of Juvenal in this poem (strophe 2, 1.8). Juvenal (Sat. 10, 219) speaks of morborum omne genus ("all kinds of diseases"); see also Juvenal 10, 188 ff.

Poem 20.

Love and Studies (Carmina Burana—No. 108; Arundel—No. 14)

The scale, in keeping with the wheel of fortune (see Prelude), occurs several times in the carmina. In this case the manuscript of the Carmina Burana provides neumes liberally. The form is that of a sequence.

1b, 7: On Dione see III, 16.

Poem 21.
A Sport with Endless Charms (Carmina Burana— No. 183)

This song is used by Orff (No. 19) for soli: three tenors, baritone, and two basses. Unfortunately the text is corrupt. We follow Schumann in arrangement but in strophe 2 prefer *lacertis* to his *desertis*. This is probably only part of a longer poem.

Poem 22.
A Song of Love (Carmina Burana—No. 174)

Orff used this song (No. 20) for double chorus. Many attempts have been made to change *hyria* . . . , without success.

Poem 23.
Girl in Red Tunic (Carmina Burana—No. 177)

Strophes 1 and 2 are used by Orff (No. 17) for soprano solo. Critics are puzzled by the third bilingual strophe (Latin and German) which does not match the first two; most editors divide the work into four strophes.

3, 1 f.: One suggestion is: *bî einer loube* ("in an arbor") . . . *an einem boume* ("at a tree").

Chapter IV, Poem 1.
The Shepherdess Says No (Carmina Burana—No. 79)

1, 4: The olive tree, unless it is a mere conventional trapping, would stamp the work as a product of the southland; the pastorals are all probably from southern France.

5, 6: Flora is a stock exotic name.

Poem 2.
Willing Shepherdess

This pastoral, by Walther of Châtillon, is in the St. Omer manuscript of his works (Strecker edition I, 17).

4, 4: The meaning of *cotulata vario* ("brightly striped") is uncertain.

This does not necessarily mean that Walther himself indulged in pederasty, although it was a widespread evil (see VI, 5). A. Jeanroy, in *Les origines de la poésie lyrique en France* (Paris, 1889), p. 280, warns us that the real life of the average medieval lyric poet has little to do with his poetry.

Poem 3.
Shepherdess Taken by Storm (*Carmina Burana*— No. 158)

1, 2: The time is April—in southern France? Perhaps an additional strophe, or more, has been lost.

Poem 4.
Shepherdess and Wolf (*Carmina Burana*—No. 157)

As in the previous poem, something may be missing at the end. In E. Piguet, *L'évolution de la pastourelle du XIIᵉ siècle à nos jours* (Basel, 1927), there is a chapter devoted to the shepherdess and the wolf (pp. 107 ff).

Poem 5.
Shepherdess Goes Forth (*Carmina Burana*—No. 90)

One manuscript (see Hilka-Schumann I, 2, p. 86) provides music. Strophe 2 is omitted there because of its odd meter, but we include it to give more point to this artless creation. The poem may originally have been much longer.

CHAPTER V, *Poem 1.*
Phyllis and Flora (*Carmina Burana*—No. 92)

This famous poem is discussed in the Introduction (p. 24). Schumann devotes seventeen pages of commentary to it. It has come down in many manuscripts, the oldest in the Bibliothèque Nationale, Paris (lat. 16208, fol. 135$^{vc/d}$), the best in the old Berlin Staatsbibliothek. I translate strophes 1–43 and 72–79. The English translation of 1595 by "R.S."—which Wright quotes in full in *The Latin Poems* . . . (pp. 363 ff.), and from which the Hilka-Schumann edition quotes liberally in its notes on the poem (pp. 104 ff.)—can be quoted here and briefly compared with Symonds and Lindsay. Symonds offers only strophes 1–12, 58–63, and 65–73 but adheres closely to meter and rhyme scheme; Lindsay does sixty-four strophes moderately well.

1: "R.S.": "In the flowery season of the yeere, / And when the firmament was cleere, / When Tellus hierbales paynted were / With issue of disparent cheere, / When th' usher to the morne did rise, / And drive the darkness from the skyes, / Sleepe gave their visuale liberties / To Phillis and to Flora's eyes."

Symonds: "In the springtime when the skies / Cast off winter's mourning, / And bright flowers of every hue / Earth's lap are adorning, / At the hour when Lucifer / Gives the stars their warning, / Phyllis woke and Flora too / In the early morning" (p. 99).

Lindsay: "Now spring had brought the flowers / and left the heavens bright, / the earth was dressed in green / and petalled red and white, / the Purservant of Dawn / had sent the stars in flight, / Phillis and Flora woke, / and saw the morning light" (p. 136).

7: "R.S.": "Hard by this brooke a pyne had seate, / With goodly furniture compleate, / To make the place in state more great / And lessen the inflaming heate."

Symonds: "Near the stream a spreading pine / Rose with stem ascendant; / Crowned with boughs and leaves aloft, / O'er the fields impendent; / From all heat on every hand / Airily defendent" (p. 101).

Lindsay: "To keep the maidens cool / a plot of trees was laid, / a spacious grove of pines / beside the runnel swayed" (p. 137).

12, 2: As lover par excellence, hero and ideal knight, he bears a significant name.

14, 1: Alcibiades had been a pupil of Socrates; he was not only intellectual, but a man of the world too.

15, 8: Epicurus (died 270 B.C.) is synonymous with enjoyment of material things.

26, 3 ff.: The furless unlined coat signified poverty and meanness; see I, 3 and 4.

31, 5 f.: Bucephalos was the battle steed of Alexander the Great; Ganymede, the cupbearer of Jupiter, denotes the squire.

33, 7 f.: Mark 10:25: "It is easier for a camel to go through the eye of a needle, than for a rich man to enter into the kingdom of heaven."

41, 1: Cythera = Venus, born of a wave off the island of Cytherea.

42: Cupid's court is described as a court of love in the manner of the troubadour conception.

72: "R.S.": "Amongst this gamesome crew is seene, / The issue of the Cyprian Queene, / Whose head and shoulders fethered beene, / And as the starrs his countnance sheene."

Symonds: "Midst these pleasant sights appears / Love, the young joy-giver; / Bright as stars his eyes, and wings / On his shoulders shiver."

Lindsay: "But Cytherea's boy / adorned that blossomplace, / wings from his shoulder grew / and starry was his face" (p. 150).

The poem "The Love Council of Remiremont," where nuns are the speakers, is similar in plot and purpose.

Poem 2.
At That Time:
The Holy Gospel according to the Silver Mark
(*Carmina Burana*—No. 44)

This type of satire became common in the sixteenth century.

CHAPTER VI, *Poem 1.*
Otto Mode (Cambridge Songs—No. 11)

Otto I became emperor in 962. Otto III was crowned in 996; in that year this sequence may have been written. (Note the inconsistent use of tenses.)

2a, 6: The Hungarians are identical here with the Parthians (3a, 2), and both are identified with the Huns.

3b, 1: A Franconian duke and descendant of the line of Conrad I.

4a, 8 ff.: An example of ethnic pride from which current nationalistic feelings generated.

4b: The Lech river (Licius) empties into the Danube at Lechsend. The battle is that of Lechfeld where on August 10, 955, King Otto I defeated the Hungarians.

7, 8: Maro = Publius Vergilius Maro: the poet Vergil.

P. S. Allen, in *The Romanesque Lyric* (p. 282), calls this ballad "grotesque" and "naked in the accentual swing of the Jesse James type of versification." This judgment is based upon an anachronistic point of view.

Poem 2.
The Snow Child (Cambridge Songs—No. 14)

This song, like 1, 3, and 4 in this chapter, is of German origin. The story told here is found in several later sources (in a poem by Matthew of Vendôme [born *ca.* 1130]), but the localization in this early version is interesting as the experience of a Swabian in Constance. Such an absurd story and fantastic legend, turned by our singer into a pleasing poem, furnished the mimes and vagabonds with welcome material. A few verbal echoes of Horace occur. Allen (p. 275) calls it

> a fabliau of irrefutable stamp which precedes the earliest French example of its stripe by one hundred and fifty years. On reading it we may recall that the comic yarns of Germany have never received due acknowledgment from other nations, although the lat-

ter have ever stood ready to suck the juice from them without a word of thanks.

He also calls it "fit for the Decamerone" (p. 277).

Poem 3.
The Lying Hero (Cambridge Songs—No. 15)

In form this song is a sequence, and has been called the first German liar's tale (*Lügenmärchen*) in which a monstrous falsehood is rewarded with a coveted prize. From its very first word on—*Mendosam*—it is noteworthy for being brief and to the point. *Puerulis* refers to the pupils in the monastic school.

Poem 4.
The She-Ass of Alfrad (Cambridge Songs—No. 20)

This song is composed in adonics. The names indicate a phonology typical of Central Germany. The action takes place in the Hohenburg convent of Homburg on the Unstrut river in Thuringia. Allen writes (pp. 279 f.):

> It undoubtedly mirrors some actual occurrence, and it conveys the impression of being an actual impromptu. Its author was either an indifferent Latinist or was somehow bound by a vernacular original, for his German constructions show through. . . . Although the author . . . strives for the epic manner and emotional intensity of depiction in order to point his rude wit, he is a good bit of a bungler. . . .

I would take issue with Allen by conjecturing that the author may have been one of the nuns.

Poem 5.
To a Boy (Cambridge Songs—No. 48)

This song is probably French. The last line echoes Horace: *Vitas hinnuleo me similis Chloe* ("Like a stag you avoid me, Chloe").

3: Archos personifies the Beginning, the principle of creation.

6 ff.: Clotho, Lachesis, and Atropos are the three Fates. The first spun the thread of life, the second measured it, while the third cut it off.

10: Thetis, the mother of Achilles, was one of the Nereids, a sea nymph.

11: Adije (Adige) is a river in northern Italy.

14 ff.: The reference is to Deucalion, the classical Noah. After he has been saved from the flood, Zeus permits him to fashion a new race of men from the bones of the Great Mother—rocks which he and his wife Pyrrha toss behind them.

Poem 6.
Consolation for the Poet (Wilhelm Meyer—No. 7)

This poem, by Hugh of Orléans, is in internally rhyming or leonine hexameters (*lirice—meretrice*). The poet is probably mourning the loss of the wench he calls Flora in another poem in the same meter and style (Meyer—No. 6).

12: See Ovid, *Heroides* XII, 208: *Sed quid praedicere poenam / Attinet? ingentes parturit ira minas* ("wrath engenders great threats").

16: Proverbial.

26: The rich man bribes the wench so that she will abandon the poor poet.

38 f.: This is a metaphor referring to the chicken leg and bits of meat which the hunter holds in his gloved hand to lure the hawk.

This and the following poem remind one of Juvenal (especially Satire VI) in their bitterness and daring.

Poem 7.
The Wench (Wilhelm Meyer—No. 8)

This is also by Hugh and is in the same meter. It shows how openly such sordid affairs were carried on in the twelfth century. It also shows how brazenly the ladies of easy virtue, who lived at home in poverty and want, took advantage of their lovers.

17: Literally, "hardly worth the fare."

30: *Tribus ovis* may refer to a coin.

33: *Villa,* plural of *villum = vinum* (wine).

35: They keep their accounts by means of notches on a stick.

42 f.:Peleus was the father of Achilles, Diomedes a Greek warrior at the siege of Troy, Pelops the son of Tantalus. The names were probably selected at random; here they are meant to represent speed.

Chapter VII, *Poem 1.*
First Request

This poem is in the Göttingen manuscript, and in the Watenphul-Krefeld edition (No. 3). It is the oldest of the Archipoeta's extant poems and was written in Italy in 1159. Of the twenty-three hexameters, 3–23 are leonine; 5–23 end monosyllabically.

1, 1: See Eccles. 3:1: "To everything there is a season." The Archipoeta uses the biblical text, quoted only in a brief snatch, to make the transition from the general statement to the particular.

1, 3: Reinald von Dassel, to whom the poem is addressed, had just been elected archbishop of Cologne; six years later he was consecrated.

Strophe 4, with only three lines, presents the plea and the reasons why it should be granted, and is the crux of the poem.

6, 1: He is barefoot.

6, 2: *Precun-do = precum do;* for the sake of pure rhyme, the poet allows himself a little jest.

Poem 2.
Jonah's Confession

Found in the Göttingen manuscript, and in the Watenphul-Krefeld edition (No. 2), this poem was written on the occasion of the court session held by Reinald in Vienne in Burgundy early in the summer of 1164. The stately trochaic tetrameters are well suited to the subject and mood of the work. In each of the eleven strophes a single feminine rhyme is used. The somber -*onum* rhyme in strophe 1 (sixteen times) serves as a peculiarly appropriate beginning.

The Archipoeta had spent happy days with Reinald; now he has been banished because of his riotousness. In this poem he seeks to make amends.

24 ff.: Jonah fled before God and was swallowed by the whale. Just so, the poet fled before Reinald's wrath, was swallowed by his own sins, and is now an outcast.

26: *Genitivus,* actually a grammatical term, is applied with grim humor to sexual excesses (see line 89).

30: A reference to the parable of the prodigal son, Luke 15: 13 ff. The reference to the swine (sow) is from II Pet. 2:22.

35: Jonah 1:7 ff. Like Jonah, the poet has deserved death; his flesh is already consumed as a result of banishment and consciousness of sin. Only his heart is still strong and free of sin, so that it remains conscious of wrongdoing.

41: Matt. 26:41: ". . . the spirit indeed is willing, but the flesh is weak."

56: Jonah 2:10: "And the Lord spake unto the fish, and it vomited out Jonah upon the dry land." As God commanded the whale to spew out Jonah, so may Reinald liberate the poet from his misery and take him into a safe port (welcome him). Jonah was pictured as bald.

59: *Vates vatum* = the Archipoeta, the poet of poets.

66: See line 52.

69: See Jonah 4:6. The King James version has "gourd," the Vulgate *hedera* (ivy). In medieval art Jonah is pictured with a branch of ivy over his head to shield him from the sun. Reinald's protection will be the ivy to shield the poet from his foes.

70 f.: The Ninivites and their wickedness are mentioned in the Jonah story (1:2). The "folk to folly bred"

*—gentes infronitas—*are the simple-minded men, with no wreath of wisdom, who tossed Jonah into the sea (1:13 ff.).

72 ff.: Note the play on *vita* (life) and *vitans* (avoiding).

81: Orestes was thought to be mad.

91 ff.: Matt. 5:29: "And if thy right eye offend thee, pluck it out."

94: John 15:5: "I am the vine, ye are the branches: He that abideth in me, and I in him, the same bringeth forth much fruit: for without me ye can do nothing." The hint is broad enough!

Poem 3.
Vision

This is in the Göttingen manuscript, and in the Watenphul-Krefeld edition (No. 5).

5: Isa. 35:10: "And the ransomed of the Lord shall return . . . they shall obtain joy and gladness, and sorrow and sighing shall flee away."

6, 4: Matt. 4:11: ". . . and behold, angels came and ministered unto him" (Jesus).

7: A reference to Reinald's love for philosophy, particularly to St. Augustine's *De doctrina christiana,* a standard work of scholasticism in which matter and ideas, species and genera, are discussed.

8: Dan. 12:1: "And at that time shall Michael stand up, the great prince which standeth for the children of the people . . . and at that time thy people shall be delivered."

9, 4: Joel 2:21: "Fear not, O land; be glad and rejoice . . ."

11, 2: John 9:24: "Give God the praise."

12: The reference is to the Italian campaigns of Emperor Frederick I, to whom Reinald was chancellor. The emperor's designs included Sicily, then (1154–1166) under the tyrannical rule of the Norman king William I. During his time no peace was possible with Frederick.

Not until the armistice of 1177, under William II, could more peaceful relations be initiated with the emperor.

12, 2: Matt. 3:10: "And now also the ax is laid unto the root of the trees."

12, 4: I Thess. 5:2: "For yourselves know perfectly that the day of the Lord so cometh as a thief in the night."

14: St. Martin, the saint of the monastery, is meant.

15–16: *fleo, fletus, lacrimas,* used seven times for humorous effect.

16, 2: Luke 6:21: "Blessed are ye that weep now, for ye shall laugh."

17, 3: The savage wolves are the nephew of the provost and his men.

19, 4: Rom. 8:14: "For as many as are led by the Spirit of God, they are the sons of God."

22, 3 f.: The Count Palatine had first sided with the hostile nephew of the provost, confiscated the vineyard in question, after it had been in the monastery's possession for a long time, and thus forced up the price of wine. This bit of levity about the price of wine probably pleased Reinald.

24, 3: Rev. 8:13: "And I . . . heard an angel flying through the midst of heaven, saying with a loud voice, woe, woe, woe, to the inhabiters of the earth . . . ," Rev. 9:12: "One woe is past, and behold there come two woes more hereafter."

25, 1 f.: Ps. 23:1: "The Lord is my shepherd; I shall not want."

25, 4: Ezek. 34:23: ". . . he [David] shall feed them, and he shall be their shepherd."

Note the artistic manner in which the Archipoeta has constructed his poem, as indeed he does all his major poems. Strophes 1–3 describe his journey to heaven, 4–6 depict this new world, 7–8 report his conversation there with St. Augustine and the Archangel Michael, 9–12 deal with Reinald's future, 13 announces a transition, and 14–16 recount his tearful intercession with St. Martin on Reinald's behalf and the poet's awakening (end of the Vision). In 17–19 he pleads with Reinald to come to terms with St. Martin and to use pressure with the foes of the saint. In 20–21 he begs for a reward from Reinald. Finally, in 22–25 he berates the Count Palatine for making the wine dearer, although the poet, a friend of the abbot, has not suffered as much as others have. The symmetrical division is: 3–3–2–4 / 1 / 3–3–2–4. Strophe 13, the axis, represents the division between the two halves. Similar symmetry can be found in VII, 2 and I, 2.

Poem 4.
In Praise of Archbishop Reinald von Dassel

This is the last poem in the Göttingen manuscript, and is No. 8 in the Watenphul-Krefeld edition; possibly it is a fragment. It is written in the "Stabat Mater" strophe. The rhyme *indiscrete—de te* has a humorous effect in spite of the seriousness of the poem. The work can not be dated.

Poem 5.
My Daughter (St. Omer—No. I, 20)

The poem begins as a song of spring but soon turns to love. The second strophe, an example of scholastic logic, stresses the principle of contrariety. What Walther means by this is brought out in strophes 3 and 4: An unhappy love affair has resulted in the birth of an illegitimate daughter. In the last strophe he concedes that this may prove a blessing when he has become old and in need of care and love.

4, 6: *relativum = patrem* (father).

Poem 6.
Complaint against the Upper Clergy
(St. Omer—No. I, 27)

This poem is found also (in part) in Arundel, No. 24, and the *Carmina Burana*—No. 8.

1, 3: from Horace, *De arte poetica* 304: *ergo fungar vice cotis.*

1, 5: Luke 23:28: "Daughters of Jerusalem, weep not for me."

1, 8: *A remotis,* from the opposite side (Antichrist).

2, 6: Acts 8:18 ff.: Simon offers money to Peter for the power to give the Holy Ghost.

2, 8: Giezi, or Gehazi, the servant of Elisha (II Kings 5:20) who was smitten with Naaman's leprosy. The term "Gehazite" was common for lepers.

3, 3: Christ's betrothed is the Church.

4, 6: Eph. 5:5: ". . . no whoremonger . . . nor covetous man, who is an idolater, hath any inheritance in the kingdom of Christ and of God."

5: Fearing poverty in their old age, the young people hoard wealth and get accustomed to luxury.

5, 5: Frugality is meant.

6, 4: *renum* (from *renes*) = kidneys, the "seat of the passions."

6, 5: Lechery and greed are the daughters of the leech.

7, 6: *Quasi modo geniti* is the beginning of the *Introitus* of one of the masses.

Poem 7.
The End of the World (St. Omer—No. II, 17;
Carmina Burana—No. 123)

1, 1: Job 30:31: "My harp also is turned to mourning."

1, 6 f.: He has leprosy; his life is ebbing away.

4, 3: These fountains from which Holy Scripture flows are the upper clergy.

5, 1 f.: The upper clergy would give men chaff instead of grain and would pass the high church offices down to favorites (*hereditarium*).

Schumann believes that before strophe 6 something may be missing, since the only accusation made against the clergy seems to be that of nepotism.

Only works actually consulted are cited.

Editions

Breul, Karl. *The Cambridge Songs: A Goliard's Song Book
of the Eleventh Century.* Cambridge, 1915.
Bulst, W. (ed.) *Carmina Cantabrigiensia.* (Editiones Haidelbergenses) Heidelberg, 1950.
Hilka, Alfons and Schumann, Otto (eds.). *Carmina Burana
mit Benutzung der Vorarbeiten Wilhelm Meyers.* Band
I: Texte. Band I. 1: Die moralisch-satirischen Dich-
tungen. (with five color plates), Heidelberg, 1930.
Band I. 2: Die Liebeslieder, ed. Otto Schumann, Heidelberg, 1941. Band I. 3: scheduled for publication in
1965. Band II: Kommentar. Band II. 1: Einleitung (Die
Handschriften der Carmina Burana). Die moralisch-
satirischen Dichtungen, Heidelberg, 1930. Band II. 2, 3:
not yet published.
Krefeld, Heinrich and Watenphul, Heinrich (eds.). *Die
Gedichte des Archipoeta.* Heidelberg, 1958.
Langosch, Karl. *Hymnen und Vagantenlieder.* Berlin, 1958².
Langosch must be used with caution because of nu-
merous inaccuracies.
————. (ed. and trans.). *Vagantendichtung.* (Latin and
German) Frankfurt and Hamburg, 1963. Many of
these translations require further polishing.
Manitius, Max (ed.) *Die Gedichte des Archipoeta.* (Mün-
chener Texte, 6) München, 1929².
Meyer, Wilhelm (ed.). *Die Oxforder Gedichte des Primas
Hugo von Orléans.* (Nachrichten von der königlichen
Gesellschaft der Wissenschaften zu Göttingen. Philo-
sophisch-historische Klasse) Göttingen, 1907.
Schmeller, J. A. (ed.). *Carmina Burana. Lateinische und
deutsche Lieder und Gedichte einer Handschrift des
13. Jahrhunderts aus Benedictbeuren.* (Bibliothek des
Litterarischen Vereins in Stuttgart, Band XVI. 1) Stuttgart, 1904⁴. Although unsatisfactory as to text and arrangement, Schmeller's work (first ed., 1847) is still

indispensable because the critical Hilka-Schumann edition is incomplete at this writing.

Strecker, Karl (ed.). *Carmina Cantabrigiensia*. (Separate octavo—publication of the *Monumenta Germaniae Historica*.) Berlin, 1926.

————. (ed.). *Die Lieder Walters von Châtillon in der Handschrift 351 von St. Omer*. Berlin, 1925.

————. (ed.). *Moralisch-satirische Gedichte Walters von Châtillon*. Berlin, 1929.

Wright, Thomas (ed.). *The Latin Poems Commonly Attributed to "Walter Mapes."* London, 1841.

English Translations

Lindsay, John. *Medieval Latin Poets*. London, 1934.

Symonds, John Addington (ed. and trans.). *Wine, Women, and Song: Medieval Latin Students' Song Book of the Eleventh Century Now First Translated into English Verse*. London, 1884[1]. New ed., Portland, Maine, 1918 (privately printed, copyright by Thomas Bird Mosher). New ed., London, 1925. I have used the Mosher edition.

Waddell, Helen. *Medieval Latin Lyrics*. London, 1947[4]. New ed., Baltimore, 1963 (Penguin Classics).

Whicher, George F. *The Goliard Poets*. Norfolk, Conn., 1949[1]. New York, 1950[2].

German Translations

Brost, Eberhard (ed.). *Carmina Burana. Lieder der Vaganten*. (Latin and German by Ludwig Laistner) Heidelberg, 1961[4]. The first edition by Laistner, titled *Golias, Lieder der Vaganten*, appeared in 1879 (but he only translated twenty-seven poems). The first edition by Brost came out in 1939.

Ulich, Robert (trans.). *Carmina Burana*. (Latin text by Max Manitius) Jena, 1927. Ulich translates twenty-nine poems.

General Treatments

Allen, Philip Schuyler. *Medieval Latin Lyrics*. Chicago, 1931.

————. *The Romanesque Lyric: Studies in Its Background and Development from Petronius to the Cambridge Songs, 50–1050.* (Renderings into English verse by Howard Mumford Jones) Chapel Hill, N.C., 1928.

Artz, Frederick B. *The Mind of the Middle Ages, A.D. 200–1500.* New York, 1964[4], rev.

Bechthum, M. *Beweggründe und Bedeutung des Vagantentums in der lateinischen Kirche des Mittelalters.* (Beiträge zur mittelalterlichen, neueren und allgemeinen Geschichte, Band 14) Jena, 1941.

Die deutsche Literatur des Mittelalters—Verfasserlexikon. Vol. I, ed. W. Stammler, Berlin and Leipzig, 1933. Vol. V, ed. Karl Langosch, Berlin, 1955.

Lehmann, Paul. *Die Parodie im Mittelalter.* Stuttgart, 1963[2].

Raby, Frederick J. E. *A History of Christian Latin Poetry from the Beginnings to the Close of the Middle Ages.* New York, 1953[2].

————. *A History of Secular Latin Poetry in the Middle Ages.* 2 vols. New York, 1957[2].

Waddell, Helen. *The Wandering Scholars.* London, 1947[7].

The manuscript was edited by Robert H. Tennenhouse. The book was designed by Sylvia Winter and the jacket was designed by Walter Denysenko. The text type is Mergenthaler Linotype's Caledonia designed by W. A. Dwiggins in 1937. The display face is Cloister Black.

The book is printed on Warren's Olde Style Antique White wove paper and the book is bound in Holliston Mills Zeppelin cloth over boards. Manufactured in the United States of America.

Edwin H. Zeydel is professor emeritus of Germanic languages and literature at the University of Cincinnati. He received his B.A. and Ph.D. degrees from Columbia, and his M.A. from Cornell.